TACKLING CARP

with

Chilly Chillcott

TACKLING CARP
with
Chilly Chillcott

Ian Chillcott

SWAN·HILL
PRESS

First published in the UK in 2007
by Swan Hill Press, an imprint of Quiller Publishing Ltd

British Library Cataloguing-in-Publication Data
A catalogue record for this book is available from the British Library

ISBN 978 1 84689 000 0

Printed in China

Swan Hill Press

An imprint of Quiller Publishing Ltd

Wykey House, Wykey, Shrewsbury, SY4 1JA
Tel: 01939 261616 Fax: 01939 261606
E-mail: info@quillerbooks.com
Website: www.countrybooksdirect.com

DEDICATION

For my wife, Lynn-Marie, without whose strength, courage and love,
none of this would have been possible.

ACKNOWLEDGEMENTS

When I set out to write this book I knew that I would need some assistance. These things simply don't happen without help. I would like to thank the following for their efforts.

Fox International and Mainline baits: their support is deeply appreciated. Tim Paisley for his words of wisdom and friendship. *Crafty Carper* editor Mat Woods: the majority of the photographs you will find within these pages are his handiwork, including the front jacket shot. Everyone at Angling Publications. My friends Adam Penning and Chris Ball, for providing the odd photograph along the way. Enterprise Tackle, Viper bait boats and Hinders of Swindon.

Many other friends have also been a massive help. The list is far too long to include everyone here, but Keith Jenkins and Steve March have both conspired to keep up my morale when the going got tough. Also, a big thank-you to all those carp anglers who have made my journey so enjoyable. Without you all, it would not have been so much fun!

Finally, thanks to Quiller Publishing for having the faith in me to pull this off and to Martin Diggle for showing so much patience when it came to editing the whole thing.

CONTENTS

My boyhood dream.

1
TACKLING CARP

As a young lad through the late nineteen-sixties and early seventies, I cycled around the country lanes a few short miles from my Bristol home. In an age where it was not such a worry for parents to allow their children to do such a thing, I chased just about anything that swam. My main quarry, however, was trout. I did not hold a ticket for any waters so, in the main, I was avoiding angry farmers and well-heeled fly fishermen. I funded my fishing obsession with a paper round, and every Wednesday morning the papers would be late arriving through letter-boxes because I would find a quiet place to sit and read the angling papers that I should have been delivering! The one person I was desperate to read about was a guy called Richard Walker. Everything the man wrote was subsequently stored in my young brain. I saved my pennies and bought his marvellous book, *Still Water Angling*. It became my bible. At this point of my life I had never seen a carp – in fact, I did not even know of a water that contained one. Strangely, the chapter about carp fishing became the most read. I have in front of me now that very book; it always makes me smile when I see how well the dog-eared pages have survived the torments of an ultra-keen and untidy juvenile. Even stranger is the fact that I did not even attempt to catch a carp for many years after I had first bought the book. It all seemed just too hard;

one particular passage has stuck in my mind over all those years. Walker had thrown down a gauntlet to me when he wrote: 'Its difficulty in capture is a spur to greater efforts and study, and carp-fishers will feel well rewarded by the capture of one or two big ones in a season; while the passing of a whole season, or even several, without such reward will cause no dismay.'

I was sixteen, taking yet another unofficial day off from school and fishing the Bristol Avon at Bath. I had just landed a small pike, and after returning it, sat on the high wall that stretched the length of the river. As I gazed into the turbulent water, I watched in utter amazement as a large common carp rolled and disappeared from sight. In the eyes of a young lad the fish appeared massive (in hindsight it was probably about 12–14 lb), and that one event was about to change my life. My 'bible' was consulted infinitely more times than any of my school books, and for the following summer I drowned any number of Walker's bait concoctions in that river. All to no avail I am afraid, but the seeds had been sown and I was more determined than ever to catch one of these mythical beasts.

The seeds had been sown.

Carp have been present in Britain for hundreds of years, but are not a native species. Probably the most significant of the stockings were by monks in the fifteenth and sixteenth centuries. During this period, groups of monks travelled from continental Europe, to join those already established in these islands. They brought with them carp to be stocked into stew ponds as a food source. However, although carp had already been accepted as a food source on mainland Europe for a very long time, I think it fair to say that, monks aside, eating them never took off to any great extent in the UK. These early imports were long, lean carp with the scale pattern of a common carp (fish of this type are often referred to nowadays as 'wildies'), and it is from this point that we can see the rise of the fish that we have come to know as king carp. I am not entirely sure how it was done, but the Europeans managed, through selective breeding, to produce mirror and leather carp. Plumper, and with fewer scales, these fish were far easier to prepare for the table.

In time, carp farming became a huge industry all over Europe and one way and another, both by accident and design, they found their way into many lakes and waterways. In Britain, too, the carp had found a foothold and were here to stay. However, carp angling as such would have to wait many more years before it really took off. Even then, it was only for the hardy souls – and there weren't that many of them.

Many early captures of carp were accidental, and examples of this can be found as far back as the mid eighteenth century. In 1907 a fellow by the name of H.S. Locksmith hooked and landed a carp of 19 lb 8 oz. This was accepted as a British record and from then on things began to change. In the early 1930s, Albert Buckley landed a carp of 26 lb from Mapperley Reservoir in Derbyshire. A few anglers began to realise that big carp could be caught by design, the most prominent amongst these being my boyhood mentor, Richard Walker. He and a few of his friends set out to catch big carp, and in September 1953 he shook the angling world by landing a truly massive common carp of 44 lb from the legendary Redmire Pool in Herefordshire. I doubt that I was even a twinkle in my father's eye when this event took place, but its impact can still be felt today. Richard Walker and his friends, having no suitable tackle available commercially, started to design and manufacture their own. Now, not only was it considered possible to catch large carp by design; anglers had the equipment to cope with them.

And while I am talking of Redmire, it would be remiss of me not to mention Donald Leney, the man who actually stocked that pool and who, more than any other, made carp fishing available to the masses. Redmire was run as a small syndicate and this meant that very few people could actually fish it. However, during the period 1925–1955, Don imported most of the carp that were brought into the UK. These particularly handsome fish were of the Galician strain and were to form the basis of this country's carp angling heritage. Their stocking in various venues ensured that carp anglers were fishing for carp of the same lineage as the Redmire fish, and other waters soon came to prominence. Billing Aquadrome, Ashlea Pool and Boxmoor in Hertfordshire all threatened to produce massive carp – and they did – but not quite big enough to surpass Walker's record. That event would have to wait another twenty-seven years. In the meantime, interest in carp angling grew, as Walker's ground-breaking ideas were gradually made more accessible.

During the nineteen-sixties and seventies the world of carp fishing was a secretive one. Anglers guarded their successful methods, and indeed the waters they fished, with alarming tenacity. One aspect that became treated almost with reverence was bait. For the most part, carp anglers had been using par-boiled potatoes, plus bread in various forms. In the late sixties and early seventies word started to get out concerning the use of special baits. These were normally created from pet foods and sausage meats. Then two major events occurred that moved ideas about bait forward. The first arose from the theorising of Fred Wilton, a very famous catcher of large carp. Fred developed the idea that a small bait containing all the nutritional requirements a carp would need could be introduced to the water regularly. This, in turn, would get the carp eating that bait in preference to all others. His results suggested that he got his theory very right indeed! However, it soon became apparent that these baits needed to be resistant to the attentions of smaller species. I am not entirely sure at what point it happened, but it was discovered that, when eggs were added to the new bait mixtures and they were placed in boiling water, the baits developed a hard outer skin. The boilie had been born – a bait that has lasted the test of time and is going as strong today as it has always done.

The second bait revelation involved Redmire Pool once again. Rod Hutchinson, who was fishing the syndicate at the time, had been experimenting with all kinds of baits, with some success. The turning point, however, happened when he started to try small seed baits. Hemp and tares were amongst those he used. These, along with some beans such as chickpeas, maples and black-eyed beans proved a complete sensation, and particle fishing became known as one of the best ways to catch carp. As with the boilie, particles have lasted through the years and still account for a great many captures to this day.

During this time, the tackle that carp anglers were using was getting better and better. The problem, however, was still how to hook the fish in the first place. Anglers knew that the carp were constantly picking up the baits, but ejecting them. Since the hook was buried in the bait it had no chance of finding a hold. In 1980 the most radical of all carping inventions became public knowledge, and that was the hair rig, whereby the bait was now attached to the hook with a short length of fine nylon (originally, with a human hair). With the hook no longer buried in the bait, it could take hold when the fish tried to eject it. To my mind, this is the single most important development in carp angling. All of a sudden, carp became catchable: what might have previously been a lifetime's worth of carp could be caught in a single season. The effect was unbelievable. Anglers were quick to notice the difference, and very soon carp became the most popular coarse species in Britain, a situation that continues to this day.

Tackle is still being improved upon and so is bait, but nothing will ever have the impact that the hair rig did. Therefore, it is rather ironic that 1980, the year of the hair rig, also saw Walker's record broken, and once again it came from Redmire. However, at a time when most anglers where switching on to boilies, the hair rig and all the latest gadgetry,

Chris Yates cast a couple of grains of sweet corn into this mystical pool. Using his old split cane rod and ancient centrepin reel he landed an absolute monster of 51lb 8 oz. Which just goes to show that there is no substitute for angling ability, no matter how much you spend on your tackle!

As the popularity and availability of carp grew, so too did related organisations. The first of these was the Carp Anglers' Association (CAA), which no longer exists. The Carp Society came next, which in turn spawned the Specialist Anglers' Alliance to look after the interests of specialist anglers. Latterly, the English Carp Heritage Organisation was formed to try to eradicate the threat of carp-related disease. This is a move that has ensured that angling can be truly represented at

Carp fishing is a global phenomenon.

government level, where the worries of millions of anglers can be aired. Magazines, dedicated solely to carp, also appeared. Tim Paisley's *Carpworld* was the forerunner of all of these, and is still the yardstick against which all subsequent publications are measured.

One of the biggest changes was that carp anglers from the UK started to fish abroad. In very pressure-free environments, carp in continental Europe had grown to astronomical sizes. British anglers opened the eyes of our European counterparts and the sport took off both there and elsewhere – so much so in fact, that carp angling has become something of a global phenomenon. America, South Africa and most countries in Europe are high on the list of destinations for the adventurous carp angler.

The biggest problem with the carp's meteoric rise in popularity was that there were not enough waters in the UK containing them. Slowly, over the course of time, this situation has eased. Now, nearly every water you find has carp in it, and carp anglers fishing it. Many speculated that the carp angling bubble would burst at some point, but I can see nothing to substantiate this. I believe it is just going to keep on growing. Thankfully, there are venues that cater for just about every desire. If

The magical world of carp fishing.

Enjoy the moment…

you want to catch lots of smaller carp at your leisure, or sit it out in the hope of a whacker, the choice is yours.

If this book is your first insight into the magical world of carp fishing, then I envy you the journey you are just about to embark upon. In this book I have covered the basic requirements for successful carp angling. I hope that you will be able to use these tactics to your advantage. You will suffer frustrations and failures, but it is your ability to learn from these that will make you a better angler. Don't be blinded by jealousy at what others have caught, but let those captures spur you on to greater things. For me, it is a very personal journey, and although I live much of my carp fishing life in the public gaze, it still remains great fun. Isn't that why we all go fishing in the first place? Read on, and I hope that you enjoy this book as much as I have enjoyed writing it.

2 CARP AND THEIR ENVIRONMENT

What lies beneath?

Carp heaven!

t is a fact that the more we understand about carp and the environment in which they live, the more it will help when we set out to catch one. All the latest tackle and baits will be rendered useless if we do not present our bait in a place where the fish are prepared to feed. To that end, in this chapter we will look at the waters that carp inhabit, and how best to get the most from the features that these waters hold. It is also worth mentioning here that I cannot possibly give you examples of every lake, river or canal, because each will have its own specific characteristics. Therefore I will have to generalise, but at the very least you will have some idea of what to look out for and be aware of.

Carp simply love features, and much of their existence revolves around utilising them for various needs. Carp are very basic creatures, with a few simple, instinctive requirements: safety, food, comfort and the need to reproduce once or twice a year. It is worth remembering here that they have been taught how do these things – millions of years of evolution has done that – and it is these factors that will have a great bearing on where the carp are to be found at various times of year. However, they say in movie-making that you should never work with animals, and that is because they are very unpredictable. Carp, despite their basic 'habits', are no different. What I am trying to do here is to give you a rough guide, but please remember that, for their own instinctive reasons, the fish are constantly doing what you least expect. As frustrating as that may be at times, it is something that makes this carp fishing pastime of ours so exciting. Let's take a more detailed look at these instinctive requirements and what they mean to us as anglers.

Safety

From the very moment that a carp emerges from the egg, self-preservation will be highest on its list of priorities. It will be at risk of predation from a whole host of other creatures, including some of the

The threat from above.

A real safe haven.

bigger larvae that will be part of its own diet in later life. Most species of fish will, at one time or another, feed on the tiny fry, including the carp themselves! As if that wasn't enough, there is also the threat from above the water. Herons, grebes and kingfishers will all take their share, and when, as the carp grow, you add to that list the odd mink you will start to see why safety comes first for the carp.

So, from its earliest age, the carp will understand the need to hide away from view. Snags are just one such place. Fallen trees for example, form the perfect safe haven and are ideal places for carp to lie up. Indeed, on many of the more snag-ridden lakes that I have fished, the carp spend much of their time there. I have also noticed that these snags hold very little in the way of natural food, which adds further strength to the argument that safety is paramount. Reeds and lily pads are other areas that carp seem to feel safe in. The tall stems and leaves break up their silhouette and help to hide them from prying, hungry eyes. There also seems to be an abundance of natural food in these areas, which obviously adds to their attraction. On any given day, and at most times of the year, these are two of the best places to find the carp. Thick weed beds will also have a similar allure. There is also one other very important aspect

Reeds offer the carp protection and food.

Weed beds hold carp
all year round.

to consider and that is angling pressure. This obviously presents a danger to the carp, and in an effort to avoid this pressure they very often try to get as far away as possible. Usually, their only option is to go right out into the middle of the lake. On smaller venues this will not be too much of a problem for the angler. However, on larger venues the carp could well stay out of casting range for long periods.

Food

It is all well and good for the carp to stay in their safe areas, but in order to stay alive and maintain their condition, they will have to eat. Many of these safe havens, as I have already said, will hold at least some natural food. It is unlikely however, that there will be enough to sustain a lake's entire population of carp. This will mean that if the carp want to feed on a certain food source they are going to have to travel to do so. Gravel

The uneven nature of a newly dug gravel pit.

The gravel bars will very often be shallower than the rest of the lake.

pits, by their very nature, have uneven lake beds. The way in which they were dug dictates just how uneven this will be. Islands, gravel bars and plateaux are formed and will play an important part in the formation of any natural food larders. Gravel bars and plateaux are sub-surface features that are raised above the lake bed and are thus noticeably shallower than the surrounding areas. The fact that they are generally made up of hard gravel means that, very often, the weed will not grow there. I also suspect that the water movement over such areas is far greater than that of deeper water, and this in turn will help to keep them clear. One other reason why I feel that they stay so clear is that carp anglers love to fish such spots. The constant introduction of bait and the subsequent feeding activity of the fish as they search for every last morsel leads to scouring of the area. As productive as these areas can be for catching carp, it has been my experience that they hold little in the way of natural food, although through early spring and summer the caddis flies spend a lot of their time there and carp love to graze on these crunchy little invertebrates.

At the base of the sub-surface features we start to find the silt. Formed mainly from decaying leaves and weed, this is the area where we find large colonies of bloodworm, shrimp and other small invertebrates that are high on the menu for the carp. Don't be fooled into thinking that this silt will be thick, stinky stuff, because in these areas the transition will be very gradual. I have found that casting even a few feet away from the gravel will, in most cases, put me in only a couple of inches of silt at worst. This is probably my favourite area to fish and there are a couple of reasons for this. Depending on the severity of the steepness of these bars and plateaux, most of the free offerings that I introduce will roll down the sides and come to rest at the bottom. Couple this with the natural food larder that already exists and it's not hard to see why the carp very often prefer to feed there. One other reason why I rarely fish on the open gravel is that many anglers love to feel safe in the knowledge that their bait is presented perfectly. Open gravel areas allow for this and consequently receive a great deal of pressure. This usually results in the fish feeding with a heightened level of caution or, worse still, avoiding the area completely!

Very often when you see carp that are on the move they will be following some kind of feature. Some lakes have very extensive bar systems and these are like highways to the carp. I am sure that they help the fish to get from point A to point B with the minimum of effort. This is useful information and helps the angler intercept the fish when they are on the move.

A carp on the move.

Islands are really the tops of gravel bars that never got completely covered by the water. It stands to reason, therefore, that their margins will be very similar to those of gravel bars and act as a magnet for the carp. Many islands have overhanging or fallen trees and these will, once again, satisfy the carps' need for safety. However, since the island margins are a magnet for carp, they are also a huge draw for the carp angler. For this reason, they will receive a great deal of pressure. There is nothing better for me when turning up to a busy carp water to find an island in the middle. It will be a fair bet that most of the anglers will be fishing to it and leaving other areas free from pressure. It has always been my experience that carp are more catchable in areas they are not always being fished for.

Islands are as much a magnet for carp as they are for carp anglers.

A carp is landed over the very spot it was hooked from.

Although some island margins drop away very quickly into deep water, it is very often the case that they drop away gradually. This gives the angler the chance to fish at different depths. Exploring these varying depths is a very important aspect of carp fishing. Sometimes it is only possible to get a bite at a certain depth, and even a foot either way may mean the difference between success and failure. Because we have the ability to fish with two or three rods it is always worth fishing them at different depths. Once the level at which bites are to be had is discovered, it is then possible to position other rods at that depth and hopefully keep the action coming. However, the same can be said of the spots that we fish even if they are of the same depth. I have had two rods fishing not more that a couple of feet from each other. A bite on one would seem to indicate that the other rod would go as well. More often than not it will be the same rod that goes every time. As I have said, carp can be the most frustrating of creatures!

While I am on the subject of island margins, it would be remiss of me not to mention the biggest feature on any lake. That is the margin of the bank that we will be fishing from. As this area is very similar to other features, such as gravel bars and island margins, it stands to reason that the bank will hold the same food sources. Couple that with a lot of discarded bait and it becomes an ideal area for catching carp. Fishing this area of the lake is not for the mallet-wielding and noisy angler; it requires a certain amount of stealth. However, the bank can be the most productive area of any lake and it should never be ignored.

So far, I have been talking mainly about large features, but you will undoubtedly come up against waters where they will be less obvious. It is at such times that the angler will have to be a little more studious. Any small deviation in depth is worth exploring here. Even the texture of the lake bed may have a bearing on whether you get a bite or not. With these less obvious features, I have always found it best to put my baits where gravel, or at least a harder surface, meets the softer silt. Ultimately, you will come up against waters that contain no gravel at all and I would describe these as silty meres. Now we have the dilemma of presentation. You see, as much as I have said that silt will form slowly as we move away

These snags on an otherwise featureless lake always held carp.

from gravel in pits, in mere types of water it is possible that you will cast a lead into some very deep and disgustingly smelly stuff. Even if the carp are prepared to feed in this, they are very unlikely to find your hook bait, which may be buried under feet of it. Once again, it will be up to the angler to identify any harder areas of the lake bed.

My most extensive experience of this kind of water has been on old estate lakes, formed mainly by damming a stream and dug not for gravel or sand, but for recreation. Lakes of this type tend to be relatively featureless in terms of major variations of depth. Once again, subtle variations in depth and make-up of the lake bed will play a large part in locating feeding spots. I have sometimes fished the firmer areas in an

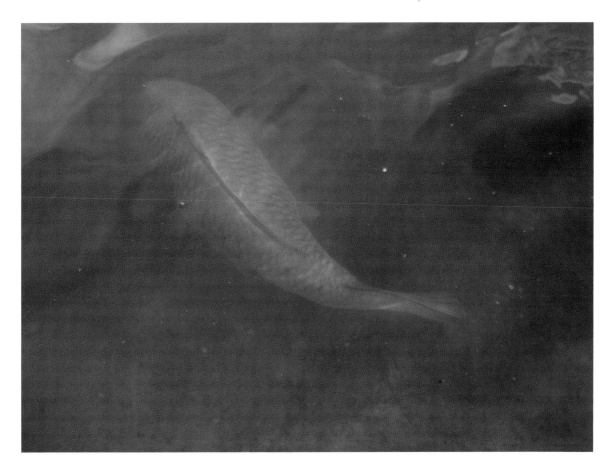

effort to make my hook bait presentation as effective as possible, but this is by no means the answer to all our prayers. Sometimes the deeper silt is where the fish want to feed and we have to be prepared to fish that too. In saying that, it is not all doom and gloom at this type of venue. Even the most barren and silty lakes that I have fished have featured snags, or at least overhanging trees. Most have also had reed beds and patches of lilies, and these will always be the first places I investigate.

Warm, sunny days are ideal for spotting carp.

Comfort

Carp love the sun, and spend much of their time just simply basking in it, soaking up the heat. On every water that I have fished, carp have been found on hot, sunny days drifting around just under the surface. Sometimes they will not move for hours on end, content just to be comfortable. If you are going to visit a water that you are intending to fish later, then there can be no better time to visit than on a hot, sunny day. You will be able to see a lot of the water's carp population. Not only is it good to know how many carp you are fishing for, it also allows you to see the size of them, and that will spur you on.

Of course, in Britain we are not always blessed with such weather and although we cannot see the carp, they will be trying to make themselves as comfortable as possible somewhere. In all but the shallowest of lakes there will be layers of warmer and cooler water. Generally, these are called thermo-climes. I believe however, that these only appear in the truest sense of the word in depths over 15 feet or so. Have you ever jumped into a lake, only to feel the different water temperatures? Well, these are the layers that the carp are looking for. It may surprise a great many anglers, but carp spend very little time actually on the bottom. They feed there obviously, but most of the time, along with considerations of safety, they are looking for comfortable levels to be at. There are, of course, ways of presenting baits to the fish that are either basking on the surface or at a certain level somewhere in the water column. These we will discuss later – for now though I think it is enough to know that they do this.

Wind has a massive influence on carp behaviour. In the warmer months, when the dissolved oxygen content of the water is probably at its lowest, the carp will head for the most oxygenated part of the lake. An area of any lake that has the highest concentration of dissolved oxygen is a comfortable place for the carp to be. By the same token, the food on which the carp feed will be at their most active too. The vast majority of the carp's natural diet is made up of living things, and this increased dissolved oxygen level has an influence on them. Also, the action of the wind and water in this area of the lake will stir up the bottom and make the food sources more readily available to the carp. It makes sense then, that the windward end of a lake in summer is the first place that I look. Many of you will have undoubtedly heard the

expression 'wind in the east, fish bite least'. To be honest with you, when the weather is warm I am not bothered where the wind is coming from, because it will have the same effect – although, carp being carp, there will always be some exceptions. Very often, for example, angling pressure will drive them from an area they would otherwise want to be in. Or, as sometimes happens, when a wind has been blowing in one direction for some time, the food sources it has helped produce have been used up and the carp move off in search of their next meal. Wintertime, however, is a totally different kettle of carp! At this time of year, in Britain, the only wind that I would consider being in the teeth of is one from the west or southwest. Winds from these directions tend to drag warmer air in and the temperature is usually a degree or two higher than normal. Carp are not normally

Wind has a massive influence on carp behaviour.

slow to respond to this. In general though, I have found that they tend to hang on the back of a wind during the colder months. And let's not forget that shallow water warms up a whole lot quicker than deeper water in winter. A very good area to keep your eye on during a bright and sunny winter's day is somewhere shallow, sheltered, and on the back of the wind. A few years ago it was generally accepted that the carp made for the deeper water during winter. I have to say that I think that theory is a load of rubbish. My ideal winter water would be a gravel pit with an average depth of 6–8 feet. This kind of water responds better to changes in climatic conditions. Remember, deep water tends to get very cold at the onset of winter and stays that way until spring arrives. Shallow water, on the other hand, will warm up quicker, and the carp will readily respond to this.

Carp Tell Us Where to Fish

We should let the carp tell us where to fish, and they are often the first indication as to the presence of any underwater features. A large part of my carp fishing is done with my eyes glued to the surface of the water. What I am looking for is signs of carp moving or leaping. There have been many reasons given as to why carp leap or roll on the surface, and for the record I would like to share my thoughts with you. Carp that are leaping clear of the water are rarely feeding fish. In the main I think they are travelling fish, moving from one area of the lake to another. And, as crazy as this may sound, I also think that this is a way in which carp communicate. What the hell they are talking about is beyond me, but I have seen other fish react to one that is leaping. Invariably this means that they all disappear to the other end of the lake. Don't you just love 'em! However, fish that roll on the surface or 'head and shoulder' send me into raptures, because I am sure these fish are feeding. My results would suggest that I am right most of the time. Any areas in which carp are showing need to be investigated and taking note of. There is a reason for this behaviour, and knowing why they are there will take you along the way to catching one.

Stock Levels

We should let the carp tell us where to fish.

In all but the most extreme cases, I think it is fair to say that the more carp you have in a particular venue, the more you will catch. With more fish, they will be easier to find and you will have more chance of seeing signs of feeding. The reason they will be easier to catch is that the competition for food will be greatly increased. On heavily stocked venues it is very likely that areas that receive the greatest pressure will not lose too much of their allure for the carp. Anglers' baits represent an

Even on heavily stocked lakes, you still have to get the basics right.

easy food source, and competing with lots of other fish will invariably make the carp easier to catch. In saying that, the angler still has to get the basics of carp angling right. Hopefully it will never be a case of simply casting out and reeling them in!

I have, of necessity, had to generalise in writing this chapter. Every water will be different, and the carp each contains will behave in different ways. There are no hard-and-fast rules when it comes to fish location. However, understanding the carp and the way in which they utilise the sub-surface features means that you have put in place one of the largest pieces of the carp fishing jigsaw puzzle.

3 RODS, REELS AND MAIN LINE

Like all aspects of carp fishing tackle, rod development has been nothing short of astronomical over the past decade. As new, lighter and stronger materials become available, so the tackle manufacturers are incorporating them into their rod design. All in all, we have never had it so good. As you progress through this book you will see that there is a fishing rod for just about every occasion: marker rods, spod rods and rods for surface fishing. I will cover these in the relevant chapters. For now though, I want to concentrate on the rods and other key equipment that we will do most of our general fishing with.

Rods

Let's look at some of the more fundamental aspects of a carp fishing rod first. Understanding what rods are all about may save you a great deal of money in the long run. Buying three rods is probably the largest outlay of money you will have to make for carp fishing. Knowing what it is you want from them is therefore essential – and not only for your wallet, but also for playing and landing the fish.

Test Curve
The test curve of a rod is determined by the amount of weight needed

The right tools for the job.

to bend the rod round through 90 degrees. Therefore, a rod that has a test curve of $2^1/_2$ lb will bend through 90 degrees with $2^1/_2$ lb of pressure. What does that mean to an angler? Well, generally, the lower the test curve the more forgiving the rod will be. Playing an angry carp at close quarters is a fraught business, and a lower test curve rod will act as more of a shock absorber. The problems arise when we want to fish at distance. The rod now has to deal with much heavier leads; therefore the test curve will have to be higher. It used to be generally accepted that the ideal casting weight for a carp fishing rod was approximately one ounce per one pound of test curve. So, for example, a $2^1/_2$ lb test curve rod would be at is best when used with a $2^1/_2$ oz lead. With the advanced materials now in use, such as carbon, Kevlar and even titanium, the

A 3^1/$_2$ lb test curve rod under full compression.

Check the fittings.

I use line clips in most fishing situations.

optimum casting weight for rods can be increased somewhat. For me, an all-round carp fishing rod would have a test curve $2^3/_4$ lb. This will have enough power to fish at fairly long distances whilst retaining enough 'give' to play carp under the tip. When rods reach a test curve of 3 lb and above, they are becoming casting tools. In an effort to gain extra yards, the action of the rod will be stiffer. Hopefully, though, by playing a carp from a long way out it will take most of the fight out of it and the lack of 'give' will not be an issue.

Length

Along with the test curve, we also need to consider the rod's length. Most tackle shops will stock rods of 11, 12, $12^1/_2$ and 13 ft. As a rule, the longer the rod, the further it will cast. However, while I don't want to confuse the issue, this is not inevitably the case. Rod length is a personal thing and very much depends on the individual using it. I am 6 ft tall and quite broad across the shoulders; therefore I can get the best from a 13 ft fishing rod. If, for instance, you are only 5 ft 6 in tall then you

will be hard pressed to get the most out of a rod of that length. While it is difficult to give you the definitive answer, I would suggest that a 12 ft or $12^1/_2$ ft rod with a test curve of $2^3/_4$ lb would be a good starting point for most people.

Choice and Fittings

Walk into most tackle shops and you will be confronted with a vast array of carp rods. Some will be relatively cheap, while others will take your breath away when you look at the price tag! What mainly dictates the price of rods is the materials that are used in their construction. Most modern rods incorporate Kevlar, but this is not cheap, and the price will reflect this. What the use of this material does mean however, is that you will be using a rod that is light, very strong and able to handle the general abuse that us carp anglers put our gear through. That's not to say that a £50 fishing rod is no good – because some are – it's just that the more expensive rods will have greater durability and better performance.

Another thing that will govern the price is the quality of the fittings. The rod rings and reel seat need to be checked. Check the whipping that holds the rings in place; it should be neat and tidy, with no cracks. Make sure that the reel seat can accommodate the reel you intend to use, and that it is not loose in any way. In fact, the overall build of the rod will give you a lot of indications as to its quality. Finally, ensure that it has a line clip fitted and that this has no nasty, jagged edges. I use my line clips in most fishing situations. I find that they help to stabilise the set-up in windy conditions and help to drive the hook home when a carp roars off with the hook bait.

Unfortunately, there are not many tackle shops that will let you wander off down to your local lake and test the rods before you buy them. So, take your time and ask questions before you part with your hard-earned cash. Word of mouth, and being the latest fashion item are fine, but rods can be such a personal thing. Certainly, try to get your hands on the rod you intend to buy before you purchase it, if at all possible.

The reel needs to cope with the stresses a carp will put it under.

Reels

Rather like the carp rods we have just discussed, there are a multitude of reels that cover many particular aspects of carp fishing. Again, these will be covered in the relevant chapters. For now, let's concentrate on the reels that we will be using for our general fishing. Carp are, without doubt, the hardest fighting of our coarse fish and it is imperative that the reel is able to cope with the stresses and strains this will place upon it. During the take, and subsequent playing and landing, your reel has an important part to play. Anglers have to have every confidence that their reels will not let them down, and to that end, quality is all-important. I have landed carp on very inferior reels, but there have been many times when they have failed me. Gearing has let me down, there have been times when the carp couldn't take line from the clutch on one of its powerful runs and, in the worst cases, I have been unable to retrieve line. Not good!

Modern-day carp reels are a far cry from the early models that we used; in a competitive marketplace, reel manufacturers have to ensure the very best quality of build. There are several factors that have influenced this. For example, carp are under such pressure these days that they spend as much of their time avoiding angling activity as they do anything else. On larger waters they spend long periods out of range of most anglers' casting ability, so reels have been developed to help cast baits further and further. Spool sizes have also increased and this helps to make sure the line lay (the way the line sits on the spool) is perfect, allowing it to leave the spool smoothly, thus increasing the distances we can cast. Also, many waters have become far weedier these days and the need to use lines of heavier breaking strain has become necessary. The larger spools help to deal with the increased diameter of the main line.

It's fair to say that the most popular style of reel in use today is one that has a 'free-spool' facility. In the early years we used to fish with the bale arm open, or the anti-reverse off to allow the carp to take line on the take. This was sometimes a bit of a hit and miss affair and tangles could result in lost fish. We then progressed to using the clutch to yield line on the take (a tactic that some still prefer). However, with the advent of the free-spool, anglers have

Large spool reels help when using heavier line.

The free-spool lever is clearly visible at the back of this reel.

only to engage a lever to put the spool into a free-running mode. On picking up the rod, the reel is brought back into normal use simply by turning the handle. These, without doubt, are my preferred reels; indeed in all situations I use a reel with this facility.

When thinking about buying reels for carp fishing, it is important to purchase one that will cover most of the situations you will be faced with. They are expensive pieces of kit and not many of us can afford to buy two, or even three, sets to cover all of our fishing needs. The other point is that it would be impossible to carry all those reels around at any one time. I believe it best to buy one that will allow you to fish for carp close in, but also give you the ability to cast to long range should the necessity arise.

In most cases, the more ball bearings the reel contains, the smoother its operation will be. Check the reel you intend buying thoroughly. If the clutch is in any way jerky, then put it back on the shelf. (This can be checked in any shop when there will be no line on the reel. Just loosen the clutch and ensure that the spool moves smoothly.) Generally, the more expensive the reel the better the performance will be. In saying that, the marketplace is getting more competitive and the prices are dropping on a daily basis. Ask advice at the tackle shop. They don't want to sell an inferior product, and should help. Look around your local lakes and see what the popular models are. Take your time before parting with your cash.

The Reel and the Take

The take from a carp can be a most violent affair. It is, in all honesty, one of the most exhilarating aspects of carp fishing. Not only does it show that you have got things right, it is also visually and audibly exciting. The alarm is shrieking and the spool is spinning at a rate of knots as the carp makes off for the far side of the lake. I don't wish to sound condescending, but some anglers haven't realised that by increasing the amount of effort a carp has to use to get that line off the spool, this will ultimately help them to land it successfully. On a lake with no weed, snags or any other obstacles that could hinder the landing and playing of

A very secure set-up.

the fish, this may not be a problem. However, things are rarely perfect. Whether you are using the clutch or free-spool facility to allow the fish to take line on its initial run, it is worth knowing that neither has to be set at its slackest. The clutch can obviously be tightened to increase resistance and so can the free-spool. On all models there is a dial that allows you to do this. The first advantage in doing so is to ensure that pressure is maintained on the hookhold. There is then less likelihood of the hook falling out. When we look at a more normal situation like weed, snags and lily beds it becomes imperative that we don't allow the carp too much line. By tensioning the clutch or free-spool accordingly this can be achieved. Please ensure that when you do increase this tension your rod set-up is such that it is able to stop the rod being pulled into the water. Make sure that the butt ring of the rod is inside the bite alarm, and that you use a butt grip that secures the rod to the rear rest.

Clutch or back-wind; it's a personal thing.

Clutch or Back-wind?

By this, I mean how should you play your fish? Both methods have merit and it is a personal choice. Some prefer to use the clutch when playing a carp, whilst others switch off the anti-reverse to enable them to yield line by back-winding. I always use the latter and it is a habit that came from the early models of reels I used. The clutches tended to be very inconsistent: they would tighten up during the fight and only give line in jerky spurts. This sometimes resulted in lost fish, and because of that I started to back-wind when a carp roared off on one of its runs. Modern reels of course, are so much better, but it is a habit that has stuck. By back-winding I have no need to make fine adjustments to the clutch and can respond instantly to the carp's sudden changes in direction. Find out what is best for you, because at some point you are going to hook a big fish and it will demand that you give it some line and respect for its fighting abilities.

Finally, on the topic of reels, the reel is probably the most mechanically sophisticated piece of equipment you will use. Therefore, it will need looking after. It is advisable to have reels serviced at least once a year, and

Keep reels clean and service them regularly.

some tackle shops or most manufacturers can deal with this. I always give mine a good clean at least once a month. I am currently using reels that I have had for many years, and they are still going strong. I put that down to the fact that I look after them. As I said, they are expensive pieces of kit, so give your wallet a rest and take care of them.

Main Line

I am going to state the blindingly obvious here. Main line is what keeps the angler in contact with a hooked fish. It therefore stands to reason that it needs to be of the very best quality. I have been using the same type of line for a number of years and have every confidence in it. As with most things, you will have to find a line you are comfortable with. The main things to look for are (a) that it casts well, and (b) it has good abrasion resistance.

Thankfully, we have a choice when it comes to what material we use for main lines, this being between monofilament, braid and the new fluorocarbon lines. We will look more closely at these individual materials in due course. Unfortunately, it is only through experimentation that we can find out what is best for us, and what is best to use in varying situations. What I would suggest is that, in my experience, the more limp the line feels and looks, the better it will cast. Some lines make a lot of noise as they leave the reel and travel through the rod rings. This is a result of friction and will detract from the distances you can cast. One point worth bearing in mind here is that, if you attempt to load say, 15 lb line onto a small reel, the line lay will not be good. This is important where distance is concerned. The larger-spooled reels tend to allow the line to be evenly and neatly distributed on the spool, and therefore the line flows off the reel more easily. Generally speaking, the lower the diameter of the line the further you can cast – but be warned. If you are attempting to cast a big lead a long way, you will be in danger of causing what is commonly known as a 'crack off'. This means that the line will break as you load the rod to cast. It is an extremely dangerous thing to happen, as it will leave a lead travelling at tremendous speed across the lake. (It *is* possible to use very light lines for casting long distances, but this will require the use of a heavier breaking strain leader, which I will come to shortly.)

Monofilament

This is the most commonly used line. Indeed, it is the one that I favour for most of my fishing. I have been using the same line in 15 lb breaking strain for a number of years now, because it suits my style of angling. However, much will depend on the waters you are on. A small open lake with little in the way of weed or snags will allow you to get away with line of 10 or 12 lb breaking strain. If, however, there are snags and other obstacles to contend with then you will have to use a stronger line. Big pits, by their nature, will require you to cast further and very often they are weedy and snaggy. This means that you will have to use line with a minimum breaking strain of 15 lb. Now, this may sound a bit confusing, so what I have done is simplify things a little. Because not many of us have the money to spend on two different kinds of reels, or different spools of line, I have taken to doing the majority of my fishing with the line that I like best. And that is the 15 lb line I mentioned earlier. In essence, I have a line for all occasions. I know that this may seem a little over the top for some situations, but I have never found that it has been a hindrance. At the very least, it saves me having to change the spools on my reels, or change lines every time I move to a different venue.

Monofilament is the ideal line to use if you have not had much experience playing lively carp. It has a lot of inherent stretch, sometimes as much as 25 per cent. This acts as something of a buffer, and it will soak up the lunges made by a carp when hooked. It can also compensate for any heavy-handedness on our part. However, that stretch can

Monofilament is the most commonly used line.

Monofilament acts as something of a buffer.

Always check the last few yards.

sometimes go against us when we want instant indication of a bite: the stretch may delay indication at the rod end. Please bear this in mind if you are placing hook baits near to any underwater obstacles.

As tough as modern-day monofilament is, it still requires some maintenance. I always check the last few yards before I re-cast after a fish. If it is damaged in any way, I will strip some of it off and re-tie the end tackle. It's better to be safe than sorry!

If you have decided that monofilament is

the line you want to use, the next thing is to load it onto the reel. Monofilament has a great tendency to twist, and this will sometimes cause problems. One problem is that it can weaken the line, and the loops and twists may make casting and setting the rod up difficult. You will read many methods in which writers suggest ways of minimising this. I am not about to argue with any of them, but here is how I do it, so that most of the twist is eliminated. Place the spool of line on the floor with the manufacturer's label facing uppermost. Thread the end of the line down through the butt section of the rod. Open the bale arm of the reel and attach the line to the spool. Close the bale arm. Using a damp cloth, grasp the line and rod just above the reel. It is important to keep the line under the same tension whilst you are loading the reel; this ensures that the line is laid evenly on the spool. Now reel the required amount of line onto the spool. To ensure that you have the optimum casting capability, you must make sure that the line is loaded so that it ends up level with the lip of the spool. This allows the line to come off the reel with the minimum of friction.

Braid

Braided main lines are a real bonus for long-range casting, and for those anglers who require instant indication when a carp picks up the hook bait. The reasons for this are that braid has a very low diameter in relation to its breaking strain, and has practically no stretch at all. I would not recommend its use by the beginner, however. The lack of stretch can cause lots of problems and playing a fish can be a frightening experience. Unless you are very careful, you will lose a lot of fish because the hook is being pulled from the carp's mouth.

Nevertheless, fishing at long range, be that through casting or by the use of a bait boat, will require the angler to have instant registration of a bite and there is nothing better than braid to achieve this. A carp making off with the hook bait on a monofilament line can move a considerable distance before the angler is aware of it: braid will not allow this to happen.

One of the major points to consider when thinking about braid is the price. It will probably be three times as expensive as monofilament. This can

Playing a carp on braid can be a frightening experience.

be very off-putting. Bear in mind though, that it is a lot longer-lasting and in most cases will last three times as long as monofilament. Thus, in the long run, the price is about the same.

Another point to consider with braid is the safety side of things. Because of its very thin diameter and texture, casting with braid can cause some quite horrible injuries. Please ensure that you protect your casting finger in some way. A finger-stall or golf glove will provide that protection and save your finger from being cut to the bone. Not nice! (NB If you buy a golf glove, ensure that it fits your casting hand – right-handed golfers wear the glove on their *left* hand so, if your casting hand is your right one, make sure that you buy a glove that fits your right hand.)

Fluorocarbon

This material has been a real revelation to me over the past couple of years. It has been around for a long time, but I never really trusted it until just recently. Fluorocarbons have the lowest sub-surface visibility of any monofilament, with a Light Refraction Index of just 1.42. This is only a difference of 0.09 from that of water. This means that fluorocarbon is far less obtrusive to wary carp than normal monofilament line. One slight drawback is that fluorocarbons tend to be somewhat stiffer than the equivalent diameter monofilament, and this inherent stiffness means that casting distance can be limited. As I use fluorocarbon for most of my close-in work, this has never been a problem for me. This material also has the added bonus of sinking a lot quicker than normal line. Add this to the use of a lead-core leader (see later), and you will have achieved the ultimate presentation in terms of hiding away your end tackle and any line that could possibly alert the carp.

Braid will last three times as long as monofilament line.

A finger-stall or golf glove will provide protection when casting.

Fluorocarbon has been a real revelation to me.

The best use of fluorocarbon is to fish it as a slack line. This is something that a lot of anglers shy away from. They feel that the fish may get away with picking up the hook bait without registering a take at the rod end. However, modern rigs are very effective, and when you bring the lead into the equation the carp is already hooked before the line has tightened completely. It is without doubt the best way to fool wary carp. Don't be frightened to try it. Once you have confidence in this method it will undoubtedly catch you more fish. My fluorocarbon main line sinks so well and follows the contours of the lake bed, there is no better way of hiding it. It is a simple operation; first cast to your chosen spot and attach the indicator to the line so that it is at the furthest drop from the rod. You will notice that, as the line sinks, the bobbin will rise toward the rod. Strip off some more line from the reel so that the indicator comes to rest in its original position. You may have to do this several times until the bobbin remains at its lowest point. Your line will then be totally on the bottom. It is a little naïve to think that carp are only swimming in the immediate vicinity of the hook bait. They will be swimming all over the area you are fishing and anything you can do to lessen the likelihood of alerting them, the better.

Shock Leaders

Many braids are so strong and thin in diameter that the use of a shock leader may not be necessary. However, many venues have banned the use of braid and we will have to look at alternatives. Thick nylon lines, whilst capable of great distances, still have their limitations. The diameter of the line is a hindrance here, and if distance is required we will have to use a thinner line. Unfortunately, thinner line will not be able to withstand the rigours of a powerful cast. The resulting 'crack off' will leave a heavy lead travelling at great speed unchecked across the water. Not only is this dangerous for your fellow anglers and other water users, it is potentially lethal for the carp. You see, if the rig lands in the water it will be fishing for itself. If a carp then picks it up it will be left towing an indeterminate length of line and quite possibly the lead. That is the worst-case scenario for me!

Depending on the conditions you are confronted with, it may be possible to use very light line plus a leader to get the range required. Please ensure that this thinner line is strong enough to cope with any obstacles you may have to bring the fish through. In all honesty, I would never go lower than 8 or 10 lb line. For the ultimate in casting performance I always use a tapered nylon leader. The ones I use come in two different breaking strains: 12 to 35 lb and 15 to 45 lb and they are 12 metres in length. The thicker end ensures that the force of the cast does not break the line. As the leader material gets progressively thinner, the speed of the lead is not hindered until the main line is starting to come off the reel. Ideal!

I like to use tapered leaders.

1. Tie a simple overhand knot to the leader material and thread the main line through it.

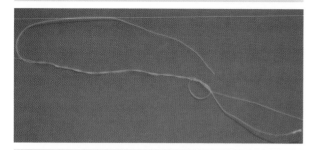

2. Wrap the main line around the leader ten times, working away from the overhand knot.

The Mahin knot is the best way to attach a leader to the main line. The accompanying picture sequence will help you to follow these steps.

The one downside of using a leader is that there is another knot in your set-up. Not only is this potentially another weak point, it also means that you will have to ensure that any items of tackle that are beyond this knot can pass over it easily. Once again, the carp's safety must be foremost in your thoughts.

Casting long distances, even with a nylon leader, can cause damage to your casting finger and, as with braid, it is advisable to wear some form of protection. A leather finger-stall or golf glove will be fine.

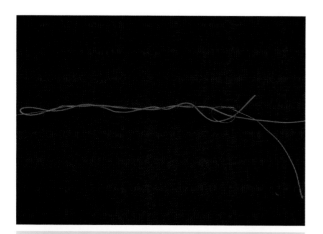

3. Now form another five loops over the top of the previous ones, working back toward the overhand knot and pass the tag end through the loop that this knot has formed.

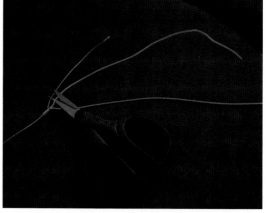

4. Moisten the knot with saliva and very carefully pull it tight. Take your time here, and use the tag end and the other two materials to ensure that the loops tighten down neatly. The finished knot should be neat and compact. Trim off the tag ends and you are ready to go.

4 INDICATION AND ROD SET-UPS

In all but the most specialised aspects of carp fishing there is no need for the angler to hold his rod all day. Carp fishing, by its very nature, tends to be a somewhat protracted affair. Holding a heavy rod and reel for hours on end will become an uncomfortable experience. I have caught many carp by simply laying the rod on the ground and waiting for the tip to pull round or for the spool on the reel to start spinning. This is fine for short periods, but again any period over a couple of hours starts to make for ineffective angling, since the angler's whole concentration must be on the rod and reel.

Casting a baited rig to the required spot should not herald the end of the angler's efforts to catch a carp. A good, stable rod set-up and good indicator system will allow the angler to start to watch the water for more signs of carp and act upon this information. With the advent of the hair rig, carp for the most part no longer give twitchy, hard-to-hit indications. The hook will be fairly well set and the carp, sensing that it has gone past the point of no return, will bolt off. This action is indicated at the rod end by line being taken from the reel. If an angler's attention is elsewhere the sound of the spinning spool may not be enough to draw his attention to a taking fish. Audible and visual indicators are what are needed here.

A good, stable rod set-up.

Bite Alarms

Modern-day alarms are a far cry from the early models. Water and electrical circuitry did not mix very well. Thankfully, technology has advanced enough for this not to be a problem any more. Without getting too much into the technology, these alarms work by having the line sitting on a roller wheel. This operates with magnets and these, in conjunction with reed switches, detect any movement. These alarms can range in price anywhere between £20 and £150, so a little thought needs to be given as to exactly what we want from these invaluable tools. At the lower end of the market the only thing these alarms will do is indicate that line is being taken. As the price increases, so does the number of functions. Crucially, you will be able to increase the sensitivity of the alarm. Basically, this means that less line will have to be drawn over the roller before it bleeps. This serves two purposes. First, you can adjust the alarm if the weather is windy; this will stop many of the false bleeps. Second, if the carp are not bolting off when hooked, the more twitchy takes will still register. A volume control will also make it easier for you to hear the alarm in stormy conditions. Third, you will be able to set the sound of the alarm to a sound that is pleasing to your individual ear by way of a tone adjustment. Some of the more advanced models produce a different tone when a carp is running away from you, as opposed to a carp that is running towards you – fascinating stuff. Finally, most of these marvellous little devices come with latching LED. These are simply lights that will stay on for 15 or 20 seconds after a bleep has occurred. This, along with using different tones, allows the angler to see which rod has had action if his attention has been elsewhere, or when fishing at night.

A lot of modern alarms also come with a sounder box. These are remotely linked to the alarms by way of a radio signal. This does not give the angler the right to wander miles away from the rods! They do help, however, if you have to answer a call of nature or if you want to turn the alarms down and use the remote in the bivvy.

The functions that this top-of-the-range alarm carries are invaluable.

Many of today's alarms come with a remote sounder box.

Visual Indicators

For nearly all of my fishing I use a visual indicator of some description. The only exception to this is if I am fishing under my rod tips. In this situation there is only one way that the carp is going to run and that is away from you, so the indicator becomes surplus to requirements. Visual indicators work by hanging on the line, normally between the reel and the bite alarm. They will show the angler which way the carp is running. If the carp is running away from you, the indicator will be tight up against the rod. Conversely, if the fish is running towards you, the indicator will fall towards the ground – which is commonly known as a 'drop back'. This still pulls line over the roller and gives a further signal via the alarm. Also, these visual indicators work by putting resistance on the line and this helps the bite alarm to give a more positive indication.

Bobbins or Hangers

The bobbin is probably the cheapest and simplest form of visual indication. I use bobbins for most of my fishing. A highly visible head is attached to a short length of chain or cord. This chain/cord is connected just under where the bite alarm screws into the bank stick. To make the bobbin heads even more visible, especially at night, they normally come fitted with a slot into which you can put a Beta Light. These glow in the dark and make it easier for you to see what is going on. I find this type of indicator to be the most sensitive, but the further out you fish, the heavier they need to be. To this end, most are supplied with additional weights that can be attached to maintain this sensitivity.

As well as registering full-blooded runs, this type of indicator helps us to see what is going on in the swim. In particular, it allows us to see tiny lifts, often referred to as line bites. These are not bites at all really, but they serve to show activity in the area of water being fished. For instance, when there are lots of carp competing for the bait you have introduced, they will very often bump into your line or pick it up on their fins. The bobbin is usually drawn upwards and then settles back into its original position. At the very least, if no real bites are forthcoming, you will be aware that fish have been feeding and adjustments can be made to bait and/or end rigs to take advantage of this.

This specialist hanger is a simple indicator, but highly effective.

The butt swinger provides a simple indicator set-up.

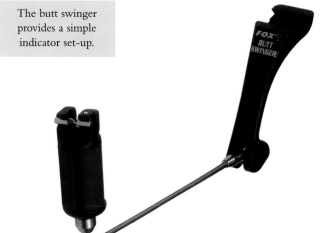

Swingers

The swinger works in much the same way as the bobbin, except that it is connected by a rigid wire arm onto which an adjustable weight has been added. This weight can be moved up and down the arm to impart more or less resistance. By sliding the weight towards the bite alarm, sensitivity can be gradually increased. The closer it is to the bite alarm, the less downward force is placed on the line and the more sensitive the set-up becomes. Some would argue that this is the most versatile system to use. The main advantage of this kind of indicator is that it is more stable than the bobbins and less prone to inducing false bleeps of the bite alarm. And, of course, you can make more subtle changes to the resistance you want on the line. Swinger heads are pretty similar to bobbin heads and can be fitted with Beta Lights for night use.

The sliding weights on these swingers increase the tension on the line.

Springer

The springer is normally fitted with a flexible fibreglass arm and with this we can impart a lot of tension to the line. This is especially useful when fishing at very long range. The tighter you make the line, the more the springer will tension it. Thus it keeps the line as tight as possible and helps to register bites more quickly at range. Because it is the flexible arm of a springer, rather than the head, that is loading resistance onto the line, the head on this type of indicator tend to be smaller than on others, but a Beta Light can still be fitted.

Rod Set-ups

As I said earlier, carp angling tends to ensure that we are on the bank for protracted periods. The rods and reels we are using are designed for playing and landing large fish, and cannot therefore be held in the hand for any length of time. Not comfortably anyway! A take from a carp can be a very violent affair and this means that whatever we use to support the rods and reels has to be as stable and secure as possible. So what do we need to rest our gear on and how best do we use it?

A secure rod set-up aided the capture of this 32 lb mirror.

Bank Sticks

Single bank sticks
allow a great deal
more flexibility.

I use bank sticks for nearly all of my fishing. These allow me a great deal
more flexibility than any other set-up. Basically, they allow me to fish my
rods in accordance with the conditions I am confronted by on any given
day. For example, if I want to fish one of my rods down the margin, I can
place that rod nearer to the spot, thus avoiding having line draping all
over my swim.

For this kind of set-up each rod will need two bank sticks. One will
have the butt section of the rod resting on it and the other will carry the
bite alarm and indicator system. There are many different kinds of
attachment that can be used to house the butt section of the rod. I prefer
those that actually grip the rod. First, this stops the rod disappearing into
the lake in the event of a violent take and second, it makes the whole
set-up just a little more stable. It is generally accepted that the front rest
needs to be positioned just in front of the butt ring on the rod. Again, in

the event of a very violent take, this ensures that the rod stays in the rests.

In most situations I can simply push the bank sticks into the ground, but not always. I have to say at this point that I don't believe there is any place in carp fishing for a mallet. These tend to be used to hammer bank sticks into the ground. Effective carp fishing has much to do with remaining undetected on the bank and hammering a stick into the ground is a sure-fire way of alerting the carp to our presence! It is also a very good way of making you very unpopular with the other anglers! Therefore I use bank sticks which have a screw fitting that allows me to screw them into the ground noiselessly.

Another way of setting up the rods is by using a 'buzzer bar'. This is a bar onto which the bite alarms can be fitted and it means that only two bank sticks need to be used. The downside of this is that it gives no versatility as to the placement of the rods and when a particularly violent take occurs the bars can sometimes come unscrewed and this could lead to lost fish.

The rod butt is gripped in the rear rest.

Another way to set the rods up is by using buzzer bars.

Screw-in bank sticks make far less noise than a mallet!

Rod Pods

Of course, there will be situations when it is impossible to drive single bank sticks into the ground and something else will be needed with which to support the rods. To this end, special rod supports have been developed, called rod pods. Most are fairly easy to assemble and are simply placed on the ground via supporting legs. Many anglers use these all the time but, as I said before, they do not allow any flexibility when positioning the rods. Some also believe that this set-up looks very neat and tidy. While I won't argue that point, neat and tidy does not always catch carp! Pods tend to cause acute line angles that at times can cause problems. If, for instance, you want to fish down each margin and a third rod straight out, the ferocity of a take on one of the outside rods could send the whole set-up flying! That said, they are fairly noise-free when being set up.

In recent years there has been a tendency for anglers to use stainless steel bank sticks and rod pods. There is no denying the durability of this material but it makes for a very heavy set-up. Lugging all that around a lake can be very tiring. I use the lighter aluminium types. Not only are they less expensive, but also they save my aching back from any further punishment!

5 SHELTERS AND LUGGAGE

As I said in the previous chapter, carp fishing can be a protracted affair. Some situations may find you at the water's edge with a rod and net in one hand and a small bag of bits and pieces in the other. However, for the vast majority of the time you are going to have to sleep at the lakeside and survive there for a while. I have to admit that, having spent twenty-two years in the Army, I can survive quite nicely with the bare minimum of kit and will put up with a fair amount of hardship. But that, understandably, is not everyone's cup of tea. In many respects, the more comfortable you are, the more effectively you will fish. Please bear in mind though, that the more equipment you take, the harder it will be for you to move if the need arises. Thus the important thing to consider is the compromise between comfort and mobility. Of course, there are times when mobility will not be an issue. On many of today's heavily pressured waters (day ticket lakes, plus holiday venues abroad being good examples), moving may not be an option. In these situations a more permanent set-up would be fine.

In this chapter I want to take a close look at all the gear you will need to fish effectively, and be comfortable during a session.

Angling comfortably.

Shelters

The most basic form of fishing shelter is the umbrella. As with most things in carp fishing, the humble umbrella has been adapted to suit our needs. Gone are the days of trying to get an old sun lounger set out under an umbrella with a central pole that was never designed for sleeping under. Thank goodness! The modern oval-type brolly has been an absolute revelation for the carp angler, having a very short centre pole to which the ribs can be fitted. Although other forms of shelter have gone way beyond this clever innovation, they are still a popular shelter, especially for the more mobile or short-stay angler. The addition of storm sides and the ability to add bank sticks for increased stability make for a very comfortable shelter.

Fishing shelters more developed than the umbrella and its derivatives are more commonly referred to as bivvies (from the military term, 'bivouac'). The next stage up from the brolly-based design is what I would call the Evolution-type bivvy. This is the type of shelter that I use

The oval-type brolly has been a revelation.

The shelter I use for nearly all my fishing.

for just about all of my fishing, and there are many reasons for this, based on the fact that this type of shelter is tremendously versatile. Bivvy orientation is always a problem, and it is not an uncommon event to have to move the bivvy around as the wind changes. With this bivvy I can simply splay the sides out a little further and this brings the front down, stopping the rain and most of the wind from making life uncomfortable. The whole thing is supported by a network of lightweight, strong aluminium poles and this eliminates the need for ribs. This in turn means more room, and I can sit and watch the water, even in the worst weather, without my back getting bent out of shape. At my age that's a bonus, I can assure you! Unbelievably, it is lighter than the standard type of oval brolly, and with a put-up and take-down time of only seconds it fits in nicely with my mobile approach.

These shelters come in a 'fully formed' bivvy design too. This is achieved with the addition of storm panels on the sides, and also a door. I have to admit that I have never used a door on any bivvy that I have ever owned. Some anglers like the idea, but I would ask you to be mindful of the time it will take to reach a rod if you get a take. This type of bivvy can be bought with a winter skin, which is basically an added outer shelter. With the extra layer, not only does this stop condensation in winter, it also acts as extra insulation.

Lastly, we come to the more permanent and robust bivvies. As I have said, these are not what I would normally use. However, as bivvy technology advances, so these shelters become more lightweight. They do take a little while longer to put up and take down, but for static and winter fishing they really are perfect. They are built to withstand the worst of the weather and you will be as comfortable in one as it is possible to be. Most come with a winter skin and a door.

The Evolution fitted with a winter skin.

A more permanent and robust set-up.

Any fool can be
uncomfortable…

Most of these bivvies and brolly systems will come supplied with a groundsheet. There seems to be some kind of macho image concerning groundsheets. Many don't use them because they think they look a bit soft doing so. But not only do they protect your equipment from damp ground, they also help to stop that dampness making you feel cold. There is an old Army adage, 'Any fool can be uncomfortable'.

Bivvy choice is a personal thing. It all depends on the type of fishing you want to do. My carp fishing revolves around mobility. If they are not feeding where I am then I want to find the ones that are, and that means moving. Carp fishing means different things to different people, and if you are happy sitting it out then you will be fine with a larger, more permanent bivvy set-up.

One last point before moving on. You will notice that I have not mentioned the bivvy pegs with which you secure it to the ground. If you get hold of the ones that screw in, then there will be no need for a bivvy mallet. It's only a personal thing, but I think they should be banned from every fishery in the world. We have previously discussed the fact that noise on the bank will only add to the carp's sense of awareness. It makes sense to me not to go smashing in pegs whilst setting up. If you do so, you will have to look no further than yourself for the reason why you blanked, and why most of the other anglers on the lake are staring at you with a certain amount of distain!

Chairs and Bedchairs

Chairs

Although a fishing chair may seem like an added luxury, they do fulfil some very useful purposes. If, for instance, you are only able to fish day sessions, then you may want to use one of the more comfortable ones. They will come with extending legs and a padded seat. This means that you will be able to fish in comfort for the duration of your short stay. If you intend to creep around stalking, then I would suggest you go for one of the lighter models. While these are not as comfortable as the larger padded chairs, they will be less cumbersome in tight, awkward situations where stealth may mean the difference between catching or not. Chairs are important here because if you don't have one you tend to start fidgeting, and when you need to be quiet, this is the last thing you want to be doing. For longer mobile sessions this kind of chair is also ideal.

A comfortable padded chair for the short-session angler.

Lightweight chairs are perfect for stalking.

When you consider the amount of gear you will be carrying, then it makes sense to have a lighter chair. They are ideal for sitting out by your rods and looking for signs of movement. The other big bonus is that if someone else comes into your swim, you can get them to sit on it. This stops them wandering around and potentially frightening any carp.

Bedchairs

Obviously, if you intend to fish overnight then you are going to need something to sleep on. Believe it or not, for many years I used to sleep on the ground. It took me a long time to realise that I wasn't on Army manoeuvres and that I could actually be comfortable. All that used to be available years ago were old ratchet-type sun loungers. Anyone who has slept on one of those for any length of time will testify as to how damned uncomfortable they were. Thankfully, once again tackle companies came to our rescue. The modern bedchair is a far cry from the torture devices we used to use! Most now come with extending legs, which will allow you to make them level on very uneven ground. Much will depend on how big you are, and how long you will be spending on the bank. I am quite a big bloke so I go for a bedchair that has three legs.

The ultra-comfortable three-legged bedchair.

In fact, however big I was, I would still go for one of these because they make for a much more stable sleeping platform. Whatever model you choose, ensure that the elastic, which supports your weight, is as tight as it can be. Once it starts to droop in the middle, you will soon be walking around like the Hunchback of Notre Dame!

Sleeping Bags

Much will depend here on the time of year that you are fishing. During the long, hot summers you may not want to take a sleeping bag at all. Indeed, I have been using just a bedchair cover for the last couple of summers. As the nights shorten however, there will be a need for something warmer. For most of my fishing I use what is called a three to four seasons bag. This will suffice for all but the coldest of weather. My winter bag is an extreme five-season one, and if I ever get cold in that then I am sure the lake will be frozen over!

Choose the right sleeping bag depending on the time of year.

The bag cover is ideal for summer use.

Make sure that any bag that you choose has a zip that works. When I am buying one, I am not afraid to get in it in the tackle shop to test it. You may well look a complete idiot, but I can assure you it's a lot better than getting stuck in it with an angry bite alarm roaring in your ear. This will also allow you to check that the bag is big enough to accommodate your size. That's important too, if you want to stay warm.

Rucksacks

Nowadays, you don't see too many anglers using these. This is because the use of barrows has become so popular. With a barrow there is no longer a need to carry anything on your back. That said, some anglers still insist on carrying everything but the kitchen sink and will need a rucksack to get the extra gear to the swim. Please ensure that any rucksack you buy is comfortable. There is little point in having the biggest one available if you are 5 ft 6 in tall, as most of the weight will be on your backside. For many years I jumped out of aeroplanes for a living and needed to survive out of a rucksack for days on end. Ounces matter when you carry your gear this way, and the way in which you pack it is important too. The thing to remember is to pack the heaviest items of equipment last. This is contrary to some of the things you may have read, but is essential and will make it easier to carry.

One situation in which I will carry a small rucksack is when I am stalking. Having the ability to carry all your bits and pieces on you back enables you to move around the lake more stealthily. It also frees up your hands to move items of foliage out of the way and to use them for climbing trees. The rucksack doesn't have to be that big because you are only carrying stuff for a short time. All that is needed is a small tackle box, a flask and all the equipment necessary to handle and weigh the fish.

Small rucksacks are ideal for stalking.

Holdalls

These are definitely the items in vogue for carrying things around. They fit nicely onto a barrow and,

Holdalls are much easier to organise than a rucksack.

The rucksack needs to be comfortable.

above all, they are a lot easier to find things in than a rucksack. I use two. One is for personal items such as tea- and food-making equipment, camera gear and any other things that make life a little easier. The other is for all the carp-catching equipment such as tackle box, carp-care gear, hook baits and some of the larger items of tackle. Above all, these holdalls have to be organised. Knowing where things are is so much better than scrambling around in the middle of the night trying to find them. Make sure that holdalls have plenty of outside pockets in which to stow things such as bivvy pegs and other items needed for setting up in your swim.

Rod Holdalls

Your choice of rod holdall will depend on the amount of protection you require to give your rods. Once again, the use of a barrow has negated the need to carry one of these over your shoulder, so they can carry an awful lot of gear. Personally, I use a very lightweight quiver type. This means that the rods sit on the outside with no protection at all. Yes, I have to be careful, but it also means that I am not weighed down with any number of rod sleeves. This works nicely with my need to be lightweight and mobile, but it may not be everyone's cup of tea, and you may want to employ something a little more robust. Some holdalls will encase the rods completely, and once they have been packed away with the bivvy and landing net handles the rods will have the ultimate protection. One other type is a form of quiver, but with individual sleeves that will cover the rods. It really is down to personal choice. Ensure though that they have enough space to store some of the other important items, such as bank sticks, storm poles, buzzers and your landing net.

The Tackle Box

This is what I carry all of my terminal tackle in – hooks, leadcore, scissors, baiting needles, artificial hook baits, tubing and a whole host of other bits and pieces. I used to use an old ice cream tub, but it got so messy. Far better, I feel, to use a purpose-made one.

For the ultimate in rod protection…

I use this lightweight
quiver-type rod
holdall.

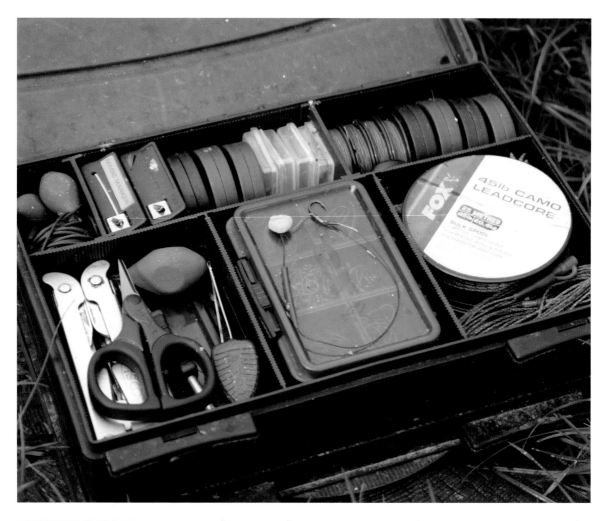

It is very important to
be organised.

Having this part of your gear organised is very important. In the daytime, this may not seem that important, but at night it is essential. Re-tackling a rod can be a very long-winded and frustrating experience.

One of the biggest problems I see anglers facing is that they carry far too much terminal tackle around with them. Leads are probably the best example of this. I have never seen the need to cart about ten pounds of lead weights around. I tend to carry that which I feel will cover my immediate needs and restock at the end of each session. Not only does this decrease the amount of weight you will have to drag around the banks, it also makes it much easier to find what you are looking for.

Cooking Equipment

Obviously, there will be a need to cook food and to make hot drinks whilst you are out on the bank. I may be an extreme example because of my minimalist approach to carp fishing. I have a very lightweight gas stove, a kettle and a frying pan in which I cook and then eat from. It's my Army training, sir! All I will say is that I will never use a petrol stove again. They are dirty, and most of all I am afraid that the smell of petrol will get on my hands and onto any items of tackle or bait that I use. This is a real phobia of mine. At the end of the day, it all comes down to what you want to cook on the bank. There are even two-ring petrol stoves available for those who want to cook a three-course meal!

It's my Army training, sir!

Torches and Sundries

Much of my formative years in carp fishing were on very small and intimate waters. It didn't take me long to realise that shining a light over the water was a sure-fire way of sending the fish out of my swim. Illumination is, however, hugely important. Not only so that the angler can re-tackle his rods at night, but most importantly of all, so that he can deal safely and quickly with any fish that he is lucky enough to catch. A head torch is the best way of using a light that I have ever come across. The fact that it is on your head means that your hands are free to deal with whatever needs attending to.

Lots of anglers have a light permanently on in the bivvy, and while I am not suggesting that this is the end of the world, I would suggest it is the wrong thing to do. Invariably it is positioned above the angler, and every time he moves he will be casting shadows across the water. At long range this may not be a problem, but if you are fishing in close you may spook the carp. These lights also tend to attract many of the night-time insects. Mosquitoes like nothing better than to home in on a bright light and invariably find all the blood they need just beneath it. There is also

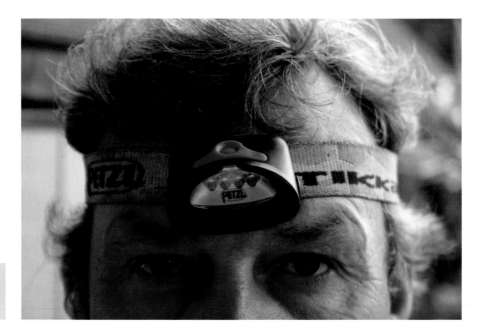

The best way of using a light.

the fact that a lot of carp anglers have the same aversion to light that I have, and in the interest of harmony please keep its use to a minimum, unless of course you are dealing with a fish.

There are also a few sundry items that will need to be packed. I spend much of my time watching the water once I have set up. To help me investigate further any signs of carp I take along a small pair of binoculars. These have proved invaluable at times.

You may get a little bored now and again, and a radio is a good way of occupying your mind, but please keep the volume to a minimum though. A book is also a good way of relaxing.

Whatever gear you decide you want to take along, ensure that it is comfortable and organised as this will make your fishing so much more pleasurable.

Feature-finding.

6 FEATURE-FINDING

When I wrote about the environment in which the carp live, I talked about all the different features that we may come across. It is all well and good knowing that these features are used by the carp on a daily basis, but how do we go about finding them? Some will be obvious, like islands and marginal features such as reed beds. Others will not be so obvious, and we will have to seek them out if we want to get the best from our fishing.

One of the most important things I do when I move onto a new water is spend some time discovering what lies beneath the surface. Not only will this information give me a good insight into likely areas in which to find fish, it will also allow me to get hook baits into position with the minimum of disturbance on any subsequent sessions. Moving onto a new water is always an exciting time. Your learning curve will be very steep, and this only adds to the excitement. On any fact-finding missions, I always go armed with a notebook and pencil. I have never found that committing things to memory is very helpful. Maybe it's just me, but I tend to forget things easily. Nevertheless, I recommend this method, and that you make a note of anything that is of interest. The next step is to take a marker rod (see later this chapter) and a good set of polarised sun glasses. You will now be ready to set off on a voyage of discovery.

Polarised sunglasses and a marker rod are essential on fact-finding missions.

Probably the biggest consideration at this stage is the other users of the water. The last thing you want to be doing is annoying the other anglers by thrashing all round the water with a marker float. Try to time your visits so you arrive when the water is at its least busy. If the venue has a closed season then so much the better – this is an ideal time for investigation, as is the winter. In fact, winter through to early spring is probably the best time to look at any features the water may contain. The weed will be at its lowest, making it easier to find anything of interest.

One last thing about these reconnaissance visits is that you will be able to go some way to confirming the things you have heard about that particular venue. After all, if you have paid good money for a ticket, you want to know that you are fishing for what you have been told will be there.

If your fishing is limited to day ticket waters, then your chances of having a good look around are going to be limited. Invariably, this type of venue stays open all year round and will be very busy. It is often the case that you will be occupying a swim because it is available, rather than out of choice. All is not lost, however, because with the correct use of your marker set-up, you can still discover what that area has to offer and thus get the best from it. Again, if you intend to fish it on a regular basis, take note of what you find in that swim. At least you will be getting a feel for the venue, and that information will be invaluable.

Marker Equipment and its Use

Rod

For many anglers, the marker rod seems to be something of an afterthought and this is a big mistake. Knowing why carp are showing at long range is a big bonus, but not having the ability to cast that far and discover what they like about that area can prove frustrating. For many years I used the same rods that I was actually fishing with for my marker work. That way, at least I knew that if I discovered something at long range, I could also get a hook bait there. But the problem with long-range rods is that they tend to be very insensitive at the tip. I found that

A purpose-built marker rod.

their inherent stiffness did not allow the sensations of different lake beds to be transmitted accurately down the rod, and this is a vital aspect of feature-finding. Thankfully these days, there are purpose-made marker rods on the market and these have made life a lot easier. I have been using one for a couple of years now that the manufacturers stated was a distance marker rod. It has all the power I need to reach long ranges, but incorporates a very sensitive tip section. Because it was built with this function in mind, it also has accurate measuring lines on the butt section. This allows the angler to get far more precise readings of the depths.

Marker Reel and Line

These, like the rod, should not be afterthoughts. Your marker reel is going to be used a lot and therefore should be of good quality. I have

The marker line you use must be braid.

also found it best to use one with a free-spool facility. This negates the need to keep continually loosening and tightening a clutch. The free-spool facility allows the angler to simply flip a lever and begin to pay line out and is much less time-consuming. Now, this really is the important bit. *The line that you use has to be a braid.* Using nylon will limit your ability to read the lake bed. The inherent stretch in this material dulls the signals that are transmitted up the line. You will be able to use a braid of 20 lb breaking strain, and this will mean that you do not need a leader of any sort – a handy bonus, since the knots in a leader will often hinder the rise of the float, especially in weedy conditions. One other bonus of braid is that you will be able to cast further and thus discover more about the features in the venue you are fishing. Remember that braid can cause horrendous damage to your casting finger, so wear a finger-stall or golf glove when casting.

Terminal Tackle Set-up

In its basic form you will set up the marker by having a running lead on the line. The next thing is to thread a rubber bead up the line to protect the knot that you will tie the marker float on with. This set-up is prone to tangles, and I have found it best to have the lead on some kind of extended link. Not only does this prevent the tangles, it also helps the float to rise unhindered.

The Float

Whatever float you use, please remember that it needs to be as buoyant as possible. It is going to have to pull a lot of line through the water. It will also need to be highly visible. For accurate depth reading, you will need to see it the second it hits the surface. Most marker floats come with interchangeable flights of different colours. This is important, since the most visible colour will be dependent on the light levels on any given day. For example, if there is a wind on the water it can appear almost white, and it would be easier to see a flight that is coloured black in this situation.

My preferred marker
float set-up.

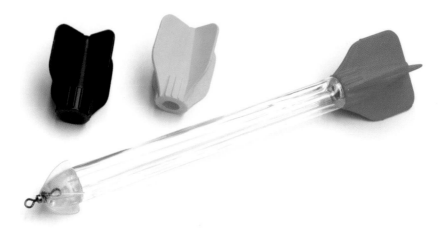

Interchangeable flights help in varying light conditions.

More and more often these days, we are faced with weedy water and it is best to use a float that is designed to deal with this. A weed marker will invariably be more buoyant, to ensure that it will punch through any weed. This buoyancy comes at a price, because these markers tend to be less aerodynamic and this will hinder the distance you can cast.

The weed marker float.

For more subtle marker float work there are smaller ones available. These can prove invaluable when fishing spots close in, where you have seen fish and are trying not to spook them.

The Lead

Using the heaviest lead you can get away with is the best way to read the lake bed. Light leads tend to skip over the bottom and do not give very good indications. Taking that point a stage further, you can use a purpose-made lead. These are made with large knobbly bits protruding from them; this further enhances the feel from the lake bed. As I said earlier, it is best to use the lead on an extending link as this stops any bottom debris from hindering the float from rising. Keep these links to either 6 or 12 in. You will then know accurately how much more to add to your depth once the float has surfaced. To make your own, tie a swivel at one end and the lead to the other. The swivel is threaded onto the line followed by a rubber bead, and finally the float is tied to the end of the line. Recently, I have been using a specially designed marker float kit and this provides all the equipment I need. The only difference here is that instead of a swivel above the lead, there is a Slik Ring and this helps the line to be pulled even more readily through it.

The shape of these leads further enhances the feel of the lake bed.

The Slik Ring helps
the line to pass freely
through it.

Using Marker Equipment

Once the equipment is all set up you are ready to go. Be careful not to annoy other anglers when you start casting around. If the water is totally unfamiliar to you, then I would suggest casting as far as you can and reeling slowly back in. You will notice differences in the make-up of the lake bed by the way the rod reacts, and the sensations that will be transmitted down it. Gravel is probably the easiest lake bed material to detect. The rod tip will shake rapidly and you will feel a sharp tapping. Silt will be very smooth, as will clay and sand. Weed tends to pull the rod round a little more and if it is really thick it will lock up solid.

One of my favourite spots to fish is where gravel meets silt. In such areas, you will feel the smooth surface of the silt then the tapping of the gravel. This is when you have to become more accurate. Using the line clip on the reel you will be able to investigate the area more accurately. This is the same for any areas of interest. If you are investigating more than one area, then mark your line with electrical tape or magic marker braid so that you can return to different spots in future. At this point it is worth noting any skyline markers that will help you cast to the spot again. A tall tree maybe, or an electricity pylon.

Depth is an important aspect of carp fishing. Knowing at what depth the carp are feeding in certain conditions will help immeasurably. Gravel areas are very often higher than the surrounding lake bed, especially gravel bars and plateaux. Carp use these features all the time as roadways and feeding areas, so knowing their location can be essential. Areas of weed will need to be noted too. Some lakes however, will have very little in the way of varying depths. It is now that you will have to be even more studious. Any slight deviation in depth could indicate a feeding spot, as could harder areas in soft silt. Find them and log the information away. As you gain more experience, these changes in the lake bed will become easier to find. Practice, as they say, makes perfect.

The last point about the marker float is that it will offer you a target for placing your hook baits and for baiting the area accurately. The basic process of baiting up, be that via a spod, catapult or any other means is fairly self-explanatory – although further details of the different methods

Cast the rig beyond the marker and 'feel' the lead down.

are given in Chapter 9. The first thing to do though is position the hook bait. The best way I have found of doing this accurately is to cast two or three yards beyond the marker. As the lead is about to hit the surface I trap the line on the spool. This has two benefits. First, the hook bait will be forced away from the lead and this will reduce tangles. Second, you will be able to 'feel' the lead down to the bottom on a tight line. This indicates further what kind of bottom you have landed on. A sharp

'donk' will indicate that you have landed on gravel, while a softer 'donk' will tell you that you have landed in the silt.

That is a very generalised look at what you want to achieve. Again, with practice this method will add so much more to your confidence.

Detailed marker float work was essential in the capture of this Conningbrook mirror.

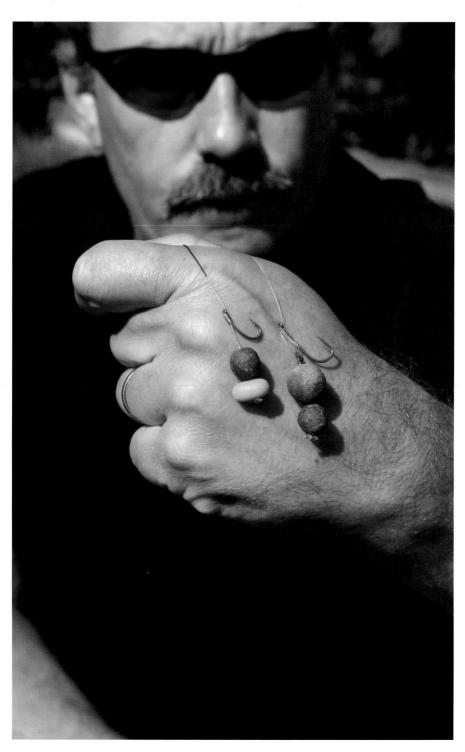

Probably the most talked about aspect of carp fishing.

7 RIGS AND THE BUSINESS END

Rigs are probably the most talked-about aspect of carp fishing. (I think it is important to say that I consider the rig to be the actual hooklink, from swivel to the hook.) Many anglers feel that this is the most important weapon in their fishing armoury. Newcomers to the sport and even some seasoned veterans believe that, if they are in possession of the latest all-singing, all-dancing wonder rig, then all they have to do is cast it into the lake and start catching. I am sorry to shatter any illusions, but this is a big mistake. Yes, rigs are an important factor, but the rig itself is only one small part of the carp-catching puzzle. The latest rigs, baits and tackle are all of no importance if you have not presented the hook bait in an area in which the carp are willing to feed, or if there are no carp in that particular area. It is sometimes hard for anglers to understand that the very fundamental angling skills have to be mastered first, in order for any rig to be successful. Locating your fish, observing them and setting traps accordingly are the factors that play the biggest part in catching carp.

There can be no doubt that, when Lenny Middleton first invented the hair rig, it turned carp fishing on its head. Anglers no longer had to hover over their rods waiting for a twitchy indication that a carp had picked up the bait. Bites now registered as full-blooded, heart-stopping runs. In some cases anglers were going from catching five or six carp in a season

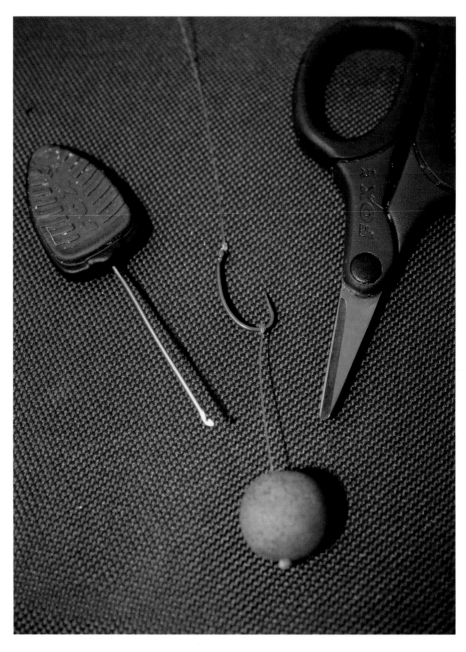

How the original hair
was tied.

to catching the same number in a single session. Halcyon days! To my mind, Lenny's invention will always remain the single most important carp fishing innovation. Everything that has followed has just been a variation of that theme.

To say that carp anglers are obsessed with rigs would, I think, be a gross understatement and the search for the ultimate rig goes on and on. Unfortunately, it doesn't exist. I have been very lucky in that I have witnessed the evolution of some of today's most devastating rigs and I can assure you that there are no secrets any more. Successful carp fishing is a combination of a great many things; the rig is simply one of them. Nevertheless, when things are not going as the angler would wish, it seems that the first thing that gets the blame is the rig. In reality it is far more likely to be a combination of many other factors. Maybe the bait is not acceptable to the carp, or your location was all wrong. There is also the fact that they may not have been feeding during your stay, or not feeding strongly enough to get themselves caught. Rigs are a marvellous, thought-provoking issue, but we must ensure we put as much thought into all other aspects of carp fishing.

It was, however, the continuing fascination with trying to improve rigs that spawned so many variations of the original hair rig. To begin with, the hair was very long (2–3 in) and for a while this seemed to be fine. All too soon though, the carp had wised up to this, and instead of simply sucking in the bait and getting hooked they started to pick the bait up with more caution. Aware that there was a problem, the fish still bolted, but when the angler struck he did so into thin air. It was obvious that the hair itself needed shortening in order that the fish picked up both bait and hook at the same time. This worked very well and it is the point from which most modern variations take their lead. The long hair rig seems to have lost its popularity, but it still has its part to play in today's carp fishing environment, not least of all when we are trying to offer the carp a different set of circumstance to deal with.

Many of the rigs that I use today take their lead from rigs that have been successful for others. Like many other carp anglers, I am continually tinkering with my set-up and it is this tinkering that will ensure that the search for the be-all and end-all of rigs will continue. Thankfully, I don't believe it will ever be found, but the very fact that we are thinking is one of the main reasons why I find carp angling so fascinating. Long may it continue!

Hooks

The choice of hooks on the market is mind–boggling. At the end of the day, choice is a very personal thing, but one thing is for sure; hooks need to be reliable in every conceivable way. Their sharpness and strength are fundamental to first, hooking a carp and ultimately, to landing it. Therefore, whatever set-up I am using, I will always ensure that the hook is as sharp as it can be. The hook is the first thing that the fish will come into contact with, and if it is not as sharp as it should be, the rest of the equipment will become completely irrelevant.

I do not sharpen my hooks, though: manufacturers with far more knowledge than I have made them, so anything I do to them will ultimately detract from their effectiveness. I do, however, change my hooks regularly. It would surprise many people, but even a short period of immersion in water is enough to dull the point. Therefore, I change my hooks every day regardless of whether they have caught a fish or not.

Ensure that the hook is as sharp as it can be.

Which Hook?

With so many purpose-made carp hooks on the tackle shop shelves, the newcomer to carp fishing could be forgiven for being somewhat confused. Rather than trying to tell you which specific hooks to use, I think it best to have a look at the styles that are available. Generally, carp hooks will be either short or long shank, the shank being the length between the eye of the hook and the start of the bend. Many anglers believe that the longer the shank the more the hook will turn in the carp's mouth, thus increasing the hooking potential. To be honest, I have never found that a long shank is any better than a short shank, but again this is all down to personal choice. One thing that I do look for is a hook with an in-turned eye. This pattern does mean that the hook will turn in the carp's mouth more quickly. The last point (if you will excuse the pun) is the point itself. Again, there are two kinds in general use, these being the straight point and the in-turned point. The jury seems to be

Hooks need to be reliable in every conceivable way.

out on this one and I have eventually come to the decision that I prefer the straight-pointed hooks for all of my fishing. Confidence plays a large part in anyone's fishing, and as much as I would love to give you the definitive answer, it's just not possible. Find a hook that you like and stick with it!

The Hooklink

Today, there are many materials that can be used to form the hooklink. Go into any tackle shop and you will be confronted by an absolute Aladdin's cave; the choices can appear endless. In the main, however, we can break these down into four categories: nylon (including fluorocarbon), soft and supple braids, strippable/coated braids and stiff link materials. Let's have a look at each category and see what they are all about.

Monofilament

This material has been in use as a hooklink for a long time and was the material on which the very first hair rig was made. The hair itself was originally formed with a hair from a lady friend of Lenny Middleton's. In order that all carp anglers' wives weren't rendered bald, the idea of using a fine nylon soon replaced the original concept. The material is cheap and readily available (our reels hold hundreds of yards of the stuff) and it was used extensively through the early years of the hair rig. Although it is not as popular as it once was, it is still fairly widely used today and is a good alternative. If, for instance, you know that the majority of anglers on the venue you are fishing are using strippable braids, then nylon may just help to confuse the carp into making a mistake. One great advance in monofilament has been the fluorocarbons. These lines have the lowest sub-surface visibility of any monofilament, making them ideal hooklink material. When they were first introduced their track record was not that good, but advances in technology have meant that the material I use today is as strong, if not stronger, than any other monofilament I have ever tried.

Our reels hold
hundreds of yards of
monofilament.

The most-used hooklink material at the moment.

Soft and Supple Braids

I believe that the use of this kind of hooklink came about because carp anglers wanted a material that was difficult to detect when in the carp's mouth. It also follows the contours of the lake bed well and helps to conceal it from wary carp. Its soft texture is ideally suited for both these purposes. It also has the added bonus of making the hook bait behave in a more natural way and anglers can use much higher breaking strains without compromising this movement. It is also tough, very hard-wearing and an easy material to work with.

Strippable/Coated Braids

These are probably the most-used hooklink materials at the moment. They are constructed of a soft braided inner with a strippable plastic coating. This coating adds abrasion resistance to the material, making it very popular indeed. However, its greatest asset is that there are very many ways in which it can be used. One of the most popular ways is to strip a little of the coating away from the hook end, thus giving the hook a lot more play. This enables the angler to retain a relatively stiff section that makes it difficult for the carp to eject.

Stiff Link Materials

These materials gained incredible popularity with carp anglers in the mid nineteen-nineties when a young fellow named Terry Hearn unveiled his hinged pop-up presentation. In reality though, the material was being used many years before this. Amnesia was the most popular of the early materials and for a long time it sufficed. Apart from adding loops at either end, no effort was being made to make the hook bait behave naturally. The rig relied heavily on the fact that it was extremely difficult for the carp to eject the bait. There are now many stiff link materials on the market and a lot of the rigs that I use today incorporate a stiff boom section of some description and they have played a large part in my fishing for some time.

Hook to Hooklink Attachments

This is one of the most important aspects of rig construction. How we attach the hook will have a great bearing on how the hook will behave once in the carp's mouth. The object of this exercise is to get the hook to turn and to take hold as quickly as possible, thus maximising the hooking potential. Some rigs are better at this than others. The term 'anti-eject' is often used when talking about the hair rig and this was what it was intended to do. Carp often suck in and blow out any potential food items and the hair rig was created to overcome this. With the bait being separated from the hook, the fish no longer had the luxury of blowing out the hook bait without the hook taking hold. As I mentioned earlier, carp anglers in the early years of the 'hair' experienced a purple patch and most pick-ups resulted in a blistering take. However, the carp, as they always seem to do, eventually thought their way around this and more and more ingenious ways were created to make the rigs more efficient.

As anglers searched for the ultimate rig, one particular style started to shape the way in which we set our hooking arrangements. This was the bent hook. Basically, this involved putting a bend in the shank of a long shank hook. Without doubt, this idea was one of the most superb hookers ever devised. However, there was a downside. Because of the bend, the hook had potential to cause damage to the carp's mouth, especially in smaller fish. Quite rightly, this hook form has been banned on most fisheries. The upside was that anglers could see the potential of having this bend in their set-up. The no-knot went a long way to achieving this, and it was simple and easy to tie. In fact, if whoever invented the no-knot had been able to patent their idea then they would have become very rich indeed, so popular is this set-up.

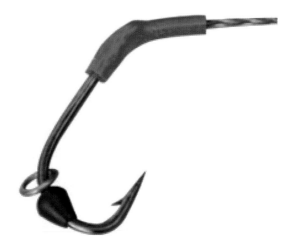

Safe bent hook presentation.

The addition of rig tubing then started to make things even better. The bend was created, and the shank of the hook could be extended, by using this tubing. Once the carp was hooked, however, the tubing would straighten out, thus reducing the damage to the mouth. Carp fishing guru Jim Gibbinson then came up with a marvellous invention, the line aligner. Instead of the hooklink exiting the tubing through the end, he pulled it through the tubing a couple of millimetres from the end. This created a severe angle and made the rig even more efficient. This is one idea that has stood the test of time and is still widely used today.

Other Elements of Rigs

Hooklink Swivels

Hooklink swivels provide the link between the hook length and the main line. I am tempted to leave it at that, but they do perform a couple of other important functions. First and foremost they make a very secure connection to the main line; it's infinitely better than tying two lines

Flexi-Ring swivels allow for more natural movement.

together. They also stop the hooklink from twisting. This can happen on the cast and, when playing a fish, and twists can seriously weaken the hooklink. The addition of Flexi-Ring swivels to the angling arsenal has made things a lot better. The Flexi-Ring swivel has a large ring connected to one end of the swivel and allows a lot of freedom of movement for the hooklink.

Tubing and Leadcore

The final part of what I would call the rig is the last few feet before we get to the lead. I think it best to explain exactly why we use tubing and leadcore. Tubing was used on the main line above the hooklink to cut down on tangles when supple braids became popular as a hooklink material. The first tubing I used was horrible, stiff black stuff. It did cut down on tangles but was little good for anything else. Very quickly, things began to change. The material that it was made from became softer and heavier. Nowadays, not only does tubing stop tangles, it also protects the fish from the main line and adds good protection for the main line when

Ready-to-go tubing.

fishing over gravel bars and in snaggy conditions. To avoid tangles the tubing needs to be a few inches longer than the hooklink. This ensures that none of the hooklink comes into contact with the main line. I have always felt that the tubing can be a very obvious bit of tackle and with that in mind I have always used the thinnest diameter that I can. This may lead to problems threading the line through it, but there are specialist tools to overcome this. As I mentioned in the section on lead attachment, the use of a tapered tail rubber allows the angler to trap the tubing, forming a seamless connection, which once again cuts down the risk of tangles.

Leadcore is a product of the fly fishing industry. Basically, it is a woven braided outer with a thin strand of lead wire running through it. It has all the attributes of the tubing, but with the added bonus of pinning the line to the lake bed in the immediate vicinity of the rig and baited area. This helps immeasurably when targeting cautious or heavily pressured fish. Leadcore has something of a bad reputation in carp fishing and a few fisheries have banned its use. However, used correctly there are no

Leadcore pins the line to the lake bed.

Splicing leadcore makes it easy for leads to pass over the connection.

problems, so once again the carp's safety should be uppermost in your mind when setting it up. There are two ways of attaching it to your main line and the hooklink and these are splicing, and the needle knot. I employ both. The needle knot is a very tidy and strong knot that allows any items of tackle placed on the leadcore to pass over it. This is vital, especially in the case of the helicopter rig. I splice the hooklink to the end of the leadcore to make it easier to put lead clips on it or, if using running leads, to allow the material to pass freely through the run ring. I normally use it in lengths of 3 or 4 ft.

A Pictorial Look at Rig Construction

Despite some tinkering with my overall set-up, I am not the kind of angler who is continually making wholesale changes to my rigs. Over the years I have managed to narrow things down to just a few variations. These are not overly complicated; in fact I strive to keep things as simple as I can. Some of my rigs have been formed to overcome site-specific problems and individual situations and some were even born out of mistakes on my part.

What follows is a pictorial look at the rigs that I use. It starts with what are generally considered basic rigs and ends with the main rigs that I use today. Remember that I use these rigs in a variety of situations and over different lake beds, i.e. silt, gravel and weed. These pictures will give you the basic idea of rig construction. There are also more specific rigs that will need to be detailed for surface fishing, fishing in mid-water (zig-rig) and when using PVA bags. These will be covered in the relevant chapters.

Basic nylon no-knot (long hair/short hair)

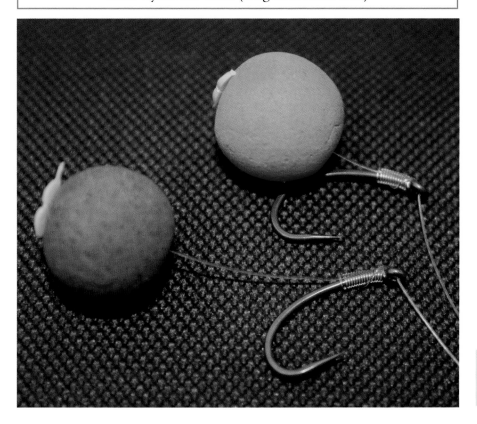

Simple but still very effective.

Basic strippable braid no-knot

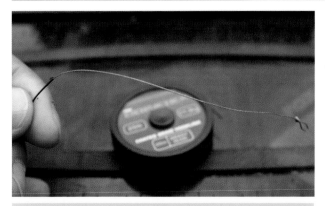

1. Strip 5–6 in and tie an overhand loop in the braid end.

2. Attach the hook bait first as this allows you to select the correct length for the hair.

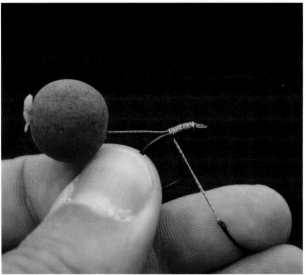

3. Once happy with the bait position, form a no-knot.

4. Pass the other end down through the eye and tighten up the knot.

5. I have caught more carp on this rig than any other.

Basic strippable braid pop-up rig

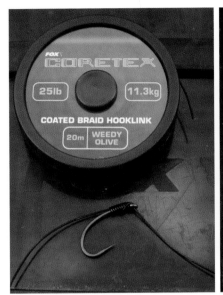

1. Without stripping any of the coating, form a no-knot.

2. Thread a small ring on to the tag end and form a loop back through the eye; blob the end carefully with a lighter.

3. A short piece of braid has been used to mount the bait; now tie it on to the ring.

4. This is how the hook bait should look.

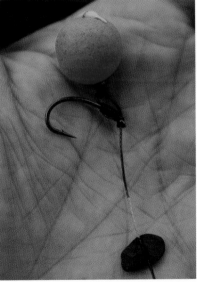

5. Strip a small section of the coating back; this is where the counterweight putty will be placed.

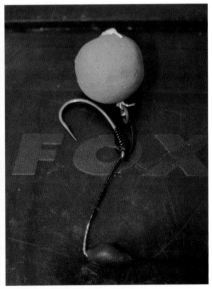

6. This is how the finished rig should look.

D-rig set-up

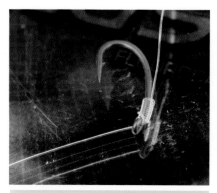

1. Form a no-knot, leaving a long tag end.

2. Slide a small ring onto the tag and push it back through the eye.

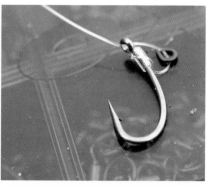

3. Trim off the tag and blob the end carefully with a lighter.

Combi-link

1. Using a 3 in braided loop, form a no-knot.

2. Make a boom section with the swivel at one end and a 2 mm ring at the other; now attach the hook section.

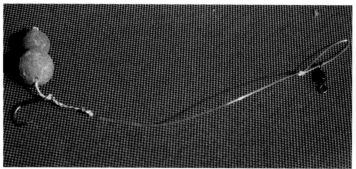

3. The finished rig: note the big loop at the swivel end.

4. These tension bars help to straighten out any stiff sections of any rig.

Stiff link pop-up rig (big loop)

1. The ideal stiff link material.

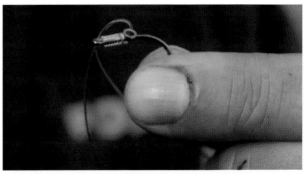

2. Form a D-rig with a small ring.

3. Attach a size 11 Flexi-Ring swivel and the pop-up link is complete.

4. Attach a boom section of about 6 in and you are good to go.

360 degree rig (big loop)

An extremely good pop-up presentation.

Leads

I believe that the first thing we need to find out is exactly what we want from a lead. For many, I suspect it is simply a means by which to get the baited hook the required distance. In essence that is exactly what leads were first intended to do, but they have now become so much more than that. How these leads are attached to the line I will come to in a while. For now I want to look at the size and shapes of leads and how important these features can be.

Again, I think it is worth looking at how the lead has evolved within carp fishing and the effect leads have had on the way we fish. For many years before the advent of the hair rig and the boilie, anglers believed that it was best to offer the carp no resistance at all. The hook was buried in the bait and you set the hook yourself. As time moved on, a lead was added to the line essentially to enable a hook bait to be presented at

> The lead is not just a casting tool.

longer ranges. Invariably, these leads would be free-running and very light, to ensure that as little resistance as possible was felt by the carp. As bait technology advanced, the paste baits progressed into the early boilie and a skin was formed on the bait to make it more durable. Before the hair rig came along, anglers were obliged to side hook these baits and thus much of the hook was left exposed. Some clever so-and-so decided that if he added a heavy lead onto his line, this would enable the exposed hook point to be driven home once the carp had picked up his bait. The first bolt rig had been born. The lead was now not just simply a casting tool; it had become an integral part of the rig.

When the hair rig did finally appear, it had such a dramatic effect on carp anglers' results that once again the lead seemed to be forgotten about for a while. Soon enough, though, the natural instincts of the carp began to take over and the captures began to slow down. A million and one different variations of the hair were invented and to some extent these kept the carp guessing. Anglers were relying on these changes to keep the runs coming and for a while the lead remained pretty much the same. Then slowly, over the course of time, the lead once again became instrumental in the effectiveness of the rig. Around the mid nineteen-eighties a 3 oz lead was considered big. It didn't take long though for anglers to realise they could get away with bigger leads, and in doing so they discovered that they caught more fish.

Today the situation has gone full circle: leads of all sizes are available and the carp have just about seen everything. The trick nowadays is to ring the changes and try to go against the flow of what everyone else is doing. 'Why', I hear you ask, 'is that so important?' Well, because it has been my experience that the more predictable we make our set-ups, the more likely it is that the carp will get away with it. While carp do not possess intelligence, as we understand it, they have the most powerful instinct for self-preservation. Each capture is logged away somewhere in their carpy minds and the more they come into contact with predictable situations, the more they are able to get away without being hooked. Changing the size of the lead we use is a very good way of keeping the carp guessing. And a carp that is guessing is a lot more catchable!

Leads for distance.

Dumpy style leads increase the bolt effect of the rig.

Ideal for fishing marginal slopes and the sides of gravel bars.

Now that we have established that a lead is not simply a casting tool, we should also take into account the different shapes of leads and their applications. Let's start with distance first.

This might sound a little obvious, but the more aerodynamic a lead, the further it will travel. Most manufacturers have leads for fishing to the horizon, and for all my long-range fishing I use what the manufacturers describe as their distance leads. Their design means that they are very stable in flight, thereby maximising the distance I can cast.

These, however, are not the leads that I use if range is not an issue. Instead I use a more compact lead. The pear or dumpy-style leads have one great advantage over their more streamlined distance counterparts in that the actual weight is more concentrated, and this increases the bolt effect of any rig. The quicker you can bring the full weight of the lead to bear, the more effective the rig becomes in my book. Now, I can cast a dumpy pear-style lead a fairly long way, but if I can get away with it I will use a flat-sided pear lead. They don't cast very well because they become unstable in flight, but their flat sides tend to bring even more of the weight to bear. They also remain where you have cast them, whereas more rounded leads tend to roll off some features such as steep-sided bars and marginal shelves.

Round leads are another excellent way of improving your rig. It is simply not possible to have a more compact lead than a round one.

They are very prone to roll around though, so I prefer to use these only on level lake beds.

Finally, the advent of the 'Klingon'-style lead has taken hooking potential even further. Based on the old clock pattern sea fishing leads, they have revolutionised much of my fishing. They remain where I have placed them because of the knobbly bits incorporated into their surfaces.

A word of warning though. Big leads can be potentially very dangerous. Please ensure that your tackle is up to the job and that you are using a shock leader. A big lump of lead travelling at speed is an extremely lethal weapon. Rods are another thing to think about. It takes a specialist rod to launch a 5 oz lead a long way, and I wouldn't want you to be standing on the bank holding a broken rod because of something I'd written!

Lead Attachment

Before I talk in detail about the various forms of lead attachment, I think it best to cover some of the safety aspects. The welfare of the carp must be your first consideration when you are constructing any rig. In the event of your main line breaking, can the lead be easily discharged from the line? If it can't or it takes tremendous effort to pull it off the line, then it should never be cast out in the first place. In this respect, the likely fate of a running lead is fairly self-explanatory; if the main line breaks the lead can simply run off the end of the lost line. It is probably the safest way to fish, but please never put anything such as a float stop or fixed bead above the lead to try to turn it into a bolt rig. This can be potentially dangerous to the carp. There are far safer lead set-ups we can use to achieve that effect.

Running Leads

I wrote earlier about the carp anglers of yesteryear trying to offer as little resistance to a taking carp as possible. The way that this was achieved was to use a lead through which the line could run easily, i.e. essentially a running lead. When the hair rig came onto the scene it became obvious that the lead was important for setting the hook. Basically, the carp felt

A standard running lead.

The safest way to use a semi-fixed lead.

the hook prick the inside of its mouth and bolted. By changing from a running lead to one that was semi-fixed the full weight of the lead could be brought to bear. This meant that the carp was pretty well hooked before the angler had even picked up the rod. That said, there are still many occasions when a running lead set-up will be effective offering, as it does, another set of circumstances for the carp to deal with.

Most modern pendulum-type leads come with a swivel fitted and it is through this swivel that the lead is attached to the line. This set-up is okay for most situations, but it can be made even more resistance free by using one of the purpose-made run rings. These large bore rings have a much larger diameter than the normal lead swivels and this allows the line to run through even more freely. In its most basic form this ring will be stopped by the hooklink swivel. Two points need to be considered here. First, the knot at the swivel needs protecting and second, there is a risk that the lead can slide all the way down to the hook if the swivel ring is not large enough. To overcome this a buffer bead needs to be threaded onto the line between the hooklink swivel and the lead.

Semi-fixed Lead

As I explained earlier, by semi-fixing a lead to your line you are bringing the full force of the lead to bear when a carp initially picks up the bait. By doing this we are no longer looking to give the carp any free movement at all. But, as I said, first and foremost we must consider the safety aspects. At all times and on all occasions, the lead must be able to release from the line. That could mean either that it turns into a running lead and will run off the end of the line in the event of a breakage, or that it can be released from the line completely. Many years ago I used to use a length of silicone rubber to achieve a semi-fixed set-up. The rubber tube was threaded on the main line and forced over the hooklink swivel. The lead could then be pushed over this rubber. In the event of the main line breaking, the lead could slide off with little effort. Nowadays there is a multitude of special beads that create this effect, which are simple and very effective.

For most of my fishing these days I use a lead clip. This ingenious device allows the lead to be held in place for the perfect bolt effect. In the event of a breakage the lead can easily be pulled off the clip. Set up correctly, the lead can even be discharged from the clip shortly after the carp has been hooked. Playing a carp is infinitely easier without a lead hanging on the line. You can now see why I like this set-up so much. The safety clip comes in two parts. First of all we have the main body. This is threaded onto the line and the arm underneath it is where the lead is placed. The second part, also threaded onto the line, is the tail rubber. This traps the lead in position and its tapered shape cuts down dramatically on tangles. The early clips had one disadvantage and that was that they could not be fixed to the hooklink swivel. This meant that the whole clip plus the lead was left running on the line with no way for the lead to discharge. Thankfully, most safety clips around today have some way of fixing the main barrel of the clip to the swivel, and it is this resistance that allows the lead to be discharged safely.

In-line Leads

I think it only fair to say that I am not a great fan of this kind of lead, but I have used them from time to time. As the name suggests, the in-line lead has

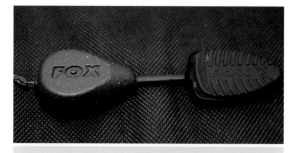

Use a baiting needle to thread thicker leader materials.

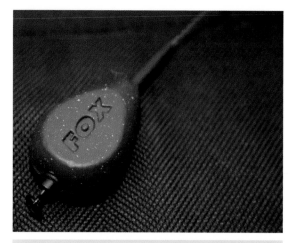

As the name suggests, the line runs through the centre of the in-line lead.

a large hole or channel running through its centre. It is through this that the main line runs. Most, if not all, of these leads come with a plastic insert. This fulfils two functions: first, it protects the line against any rough edges inside the lead and second, it allows the hooklink swivel to be trapped in the front end of the lead. This makes it a semi-fixed set-up. The inclusion of a tapered tail rubber at the back of the lead once again cuts down on tangles. The reason I don't use them much is that they have a tendency to wobble in flight, and the thought of the lead hitting the bottom nose first and damaging the hooklink swivel doesn't fill me with too much confidence. They do have a place in my fishing though and I will cover this in subsequent chapters.

Helicopter Rigs

The helicopter rig, or rotary rig as some call it, was designed with a specific purpose in mind. That was to enable very long casts to be

If you are not sure how to make a safe helicopter rig then it would be best to buy a ready-tied one.

made without the worry that the rig would be tangled. Remember, the longer a rig is in flight, the greater the chance of it tangling.

Instead of the hooklink being attached to the end of the main line, the helicopter rig has the lead on the end of the line and the hooklink is allowed to rotate around that. Many fishery owners have banned the use of this rig because it is often used in a very dangerous way. To my mind though, once it is set up correctly it is the safest way to fish. With any other set-up, once the main line breaks the fish is left towing line. With this rig all the fish ends up with is the hooklink. So let's have a look at how to get the safest set-up we can.

As I have already said, this rig was designed to cast a single hook bait a very long way, and to fish it safely I don't believe that you can use it with PVA bags or stringers (which are discussed in Chapter 11). The resistance caused by these will drag the hooklink up the line and dislodge the top stopper bead. Because of this, anglers have taken to fixing this stopper bead permanently in place, which is a very dangerous thing to do. If the stopper cannot slip up the line then a breakage in the main line will leave a fish permanently tethered to the lead and this can easily result in its death. If you want to use PVA products then please do so with another lead set-up. The carp's safety must always come first!

As I said at the beginning of this chapter, rigs are not the be-all and end-all of carp fishing. The fact that the rig is the first thing that the carp will come into contact with, however, means that you need to get this area as right as you can. If the rig is ineffective or is frightening the carp away, this means that all the rest of your gear is immaterial. *Please always think of the carp's safety.* Sorry to labour this point, but every effort must be made to protect these pressured fish.

8 BAITS FOR CARP

Pick up any one of the weekly angling magazines and you will see that carp have been caught on a whole host of different baits. To the newcomer to carp fishing this must seem hugely confusing. But don't worry, because I don't think there is a carp angler alive who hasn't gone through this confusion at one point or another. You will be in good company. For me, this is one of the most fascinating aspects of our sport.

It can all seem a bit confusing…

What bait to use, and just as importantly, how to use it? Over the years I have tried just about every kind of bait imaginable. Some have been useless, some have had limited success, while others are, and continue to be, very good indeed. Unfortunately, the only way you can come to these conclusions is through experience, and that cannot be bought from a tackle shop. By taking a look at the individual baits, we will be able to see what is available and how we can get the best from them. (It would be impossible for me to include every bait that has been used to catch a carp, so we will concentrate on those that I have used.)

General Thoughts on Bait and Pre-baiting

I don't know about you, but talk of splitting enzymes, amino acids and other pearls of the bait-making science tends to put me to sleep. Also, bait companies never include the recipe for their baits on the packaging, so catch reports, word of mouth and experience will have to guide us for the most part. The bottom line is that there is little doubt that some baits are much better than others, for one reason or another. The baits that I use are, as far as I am concerned, the best I can possibly use. I no longer have to think about what the ingredients are and this allows me concentrate more on other important aspects of carp fishing. I have used the same bait company for the past fourteen years; their thoughts on bait are pretty similar to mine. Not being blinded by science, I have been able to concentrate on using their bait to best effect, and what I have learnt has been a real eye-opener, I can tell you!

I have long held the belief that bait, and how it is applied to the water, is just as important as any rig. So, like most anglers, I have many thoughts on bait floating around in my head, but every time I really examine what I want to use a bait for, and what I want to achieve, I come to the same conclusion. I want a bait that the carp will keep on eating because they enjoy it, and one that is also doing them good. The upside of using a bait like this is that they will continue to lower their natural defences, and in doing so become vastly more catchable. To achieve this level of preoccupation, however, requires a degree of hard work and this is something that some anglers shy away from. Not to put too fine a point

Good quality bait has kept this stunning 35 lb common carp in mint condition.

on it, if you are not prepared to apply a bait properly, then you will struggle to get the best from it. And therein lies the first hurdle.

I have said on many occasions that carp fishing is many different things to many different people. For some, it is an escape from the rigours of everyday life; a carp caught being a bonus. Others work as hard as life's various limitations will allow, whilst others will stop at nothing to achieve their targets. You, as an individual, will have to weigh up the kind of fishing you will be doing. Think seriously about the following points. How much time have you got at your disposal? How much bait can you afford to use? How much pressure are the carp under, and how many carp are you fishing for? What bait or baits have been successful in the past? How much bait are the carp used to seeing? There is a whole host of other things to think about, but I don't want to confuse the issue here. Once you have established the parameters under which you will be fishing, you will be able to make a more informed choice.

As I commented at the start of this chapter, I will take a more detailed look at the individual baits in a while. For now, I want to make some general points about the main baits that I use, and why and how I use them. Boilies are my preferred choice of bait for carp fishing. From time to time I back these up with other well-known carp-catchers, but as boilies are probably the most popular bait in use today I will start with them.

When boilies became commercially available quite a few years ago, they were viewed by many as cheating, or a cop-out. Anglers were no longer in control of the ingredients their baits contained. Time marches on and ready-made or shelf-life boilies are now an accepted part of carp fishing. Because they may be stored on a tackle shop shelf for a long time they need to have preservatives added to prolong their life. It is generally accepted that they include ingredients that are not that high in food value and rely heavily on the liquid attractors that they contain. Because of that, they have no place in my carp fishing. Now that is a bit of a sweeping statement, and one that I suspect some will disagree with. But for many years I have been applying boilies to numerous waters, and from my experience I can tell you that the higher the food quality of the bait, the longer its lifespan will be in terms of catching carp. Ready-mades are designed in the main to get the attention of the fish, and by having high levels of attraction they elicit a feeding response. The trouble is, it doesn't take long for the carp to suss out that they lack the necessary quality to maintain a healthy lifestyle. Let me put that another way. If you went to the local burger joint for every one of your meals it wouldn't be long before you were in a bit of a state. I hope you see what I am trying to say here. For shelf-life boilies I read attractor baits, and I am sure that it is this high level of attraction that makes it so easy for the carp to recognise the inherent dangers. However, although I don't personally use them, they do have a place: for the angler who is working on a limited time budget they can prove invaluable. As I said, by their very nature they get the attention of the carp quickly and this, in itself, may be enough for the short-stay angler to get takes.

Carp eat food and lots of it! Of that there can be little doubt. The

Designed to get the carp's attention.

better quality that food is, the more good it will do the fish and the more likely they are to eat it. The longer stay angler, or one who can visit a chosen venue more regularly, must take this into account. It is only fair to say that I have more time than most carp anglers so I am looking to apply a bait for the long term. I am not fazed if it takes a while for them to respond. The bait I use is of the best quality and I know that they will eventually switch on to it. More often than not though, I don't have to wait too long. Using the same kind of baits for fourteen years now has allowed me to see that they give off such good food signals that they have a somewhat instant appeal and will also keep on catching for as long as I want them to. I have always found that the carp simply love the stuff and will get caught on it time and again. You, also, will have to find a bait that you are confident in, and one that the fish want to eat, then set about making it available to them as often as possible. Remember, the more they see of it without getting caught on it, the more confident they will be. The more confident they are, the more likely you are to catch them.

The quantity of bait used is an interesting aspect. There will be those amongst you who have read of the amount of bait that I use from time to time and, no doubt, some of you will be thinking, 'It's all right for him, he gets it free.' I'll not dispute that, but this is in the context of testing new and prototype baits for a bait company, to find out how effective they are before they are sold to the public. Yes, this may be to my advantage, but it's worth saying again – carp eat food and lots of it. It would surprise a great many anglers just how much a carp can eat in a single sitting. You will have to take my word for that, unless you have witnessed otherwise, but by knowing that fact you can adjust your own fishing accordingly. I often use the following analogy to get my point across. Formula One racing drivers roar around racetracks in cars loaded with all the latest high-tech gadgetry. This is something that the average

A 41lb mirror taken after establishing my bait.

driver will never be able to do. The reason why the car manufacturers plough huge amounts of money into the sport is that they can transfer much of the data and technology into the cars that we drive on the roads. This doesn't mean that we can drive around at 200 mph; it just means that the vehicle that you are driving is as reliable as it can be, and won't let you down. Now, while I would never consider myself the Michael Schumacher of carp fishing, writing about my findings will hopefully give anglers a better understanding of the carp they are trying to catch. And the more you understand, the more likely you are to catch them. Knowledge is power!

What a wonderful sales pitch it would be if I were to say that all you have to do is buy a ton of quality bait, throw it in the pond, sit back and start to reel them in. There is much more to it than that. Large quantities of bait work, but by far the most important aspects of bait application are the regularity with which you put it in and where you put it.

Having selected the venue you intend to fish, you then have to think about the bait you want to use. If you have one that you are already confident in, then there is little need to change although, if the water has a history of one or more particular baits being successful, it would then make sense to consider using one of those. After all, much of the baiting-up is being done by other anglers! Personally, however, I prefer to get my own bait established, and then when the results start coming the rewards are far more satisfying.

If your chosen water has a closed season, then so much the better. Carp behave differently when they are not being fished for all the time. Invariably, they are more visible and this will allow you to identify most of the areas they are visiting. I have lost count of the number of times I have arrived at a water for the start of a new season, to be confronted with carp showing everywhere. Then, once the leads and lines start hitting the water, they miraculously disappear. The closed season will allow you to apply bait when there is no pressure on the fish, and their confidence will be gained much more quickly. On the other hand, if the water remains open all year round, then you will be establishing the bait whilst you are fishing.

Overall, I try to get bait into as many of the productive spots as I can. By doing this I am not too bothered if one of the spots is being fished, because hopefully one of the others is not. Even if you have to fish an area that you have not baited, hopefully by then the fish will recognise your bait wherever you put it. It constantly amazes me when I hear anglers who can only fish, say, at the weekend complain that they cannot compete with anglers who have more time. You can, but it takes a little sacrifice. If you only have a Friday and Saturday night available there is a way of increasing your session. Instead of visiting the local pub on a Wednesday night, why not go to the lake and put some bait in? Not lots, say fifty or sixty baits on your chosen spots. That bait is then working for you until you arrive. Your session is now four days long. Another added bonus arising from this is that you will be more in touch with what is happening at the lake. This sort of knowledge can be invaluable when you think about your time on the bank. If it is possible that you could bait up every other day, then you will have bait in the water all week long. There is no doubt that others will catch carp because of your hard work, but if you stick to it you will invariably get the lion's share. It all depends on how badly you want it.

In the main, I have been talking so far about boilies, as they seem to be the most popular bait in use today. They are, however, not the only option we have, so let's take a look at what else is available. Trout pellets in all their various forms have had a massive impact on carp fishing for as long as I can remember. Since they were first used to make paste their acceptability to carp cannot be ignored. However, I rarely use standard pellets these days, preferring those that carry the same food signals as the boilies I am using. They are ideal for pre-baiting. Pellets are also relatively inexpensive, and this means that they are a great favourite with carp anglers. There are ways of making them a little more exciting, and we will take a look at this in a while.

Particle baits also need little in the way of introduction. They have been in use for a very long time. Probably the most popular bait of this kind is hemp, and I will use this as my main example. It's best not to forget the other seeds and pulses though: chickpeas, maples, maize, corn, groats, tares and the ever-popular multi-seed mixes such as Parti-Blend and pigeon conditioner. I won't go into the details of their preparation at the moment, but a word of warning first. In their natural state these kinds of baits represent a danger to the carp. In the main, they are indigestible and some kind of boiling will be needed before they can be introduced to the lake. If you have any doubts then please ask for advice from the supplier or the retailer. The boiling process ensures that they are not harmful to the carp. They are also infinitely more attractive and edible once they have been soaked and boiled, as this process releases their natural oils, sugars and flavours.

My favourite combination.

Hemp is one of the most awesome carp attractors of all time. Its use often results in the carp becoming totally preoccupied on it, which is what we are trying to achieve with the use of particle baits. The downside of this is that it can be difficult to get a bite when using other baits over the top of it. What seems to happen is that the carp get so engrossed in finding every last seed, that they often ignore other food items in the baited area. One thing is for sure though. If you want to attract carp into your area and keep them there, hemp will do just that. Cheap and easy to prepare, I find it is best when used in conjunction with other baits – my favourite combination is boilies and pellets. Hemp is very instantaneous and needs little in the way of pre-baiting, but it is still a good idea to introduce some onto your spots as often as you can. Make sure that you add some larger food items at the same time, just to get them used to seeing and eating it.

To be honest with you, I have always viewed nuts with a certain amount of suspicion, although there is no doubt that carp absolutely love them. Used in moderation little can go wrong, but because they are classed as a particle bait, they tend to be introduced at needlessly high levels. In extreme cases their use on some waters has led to the fish losing weight and becoming out of condition, so please be very careful when using them. As with seed baits, they will need to be prepared properly and again I will cover this in a while. Yet again, the boiling process allows the nuts to become more digestible and attractive for the carp. Over the years I have used many different kinds: Brazil nuts, hazel nuts, almonds, peanuts and tiger nuts. All of these have brought varying degrees of success, but I have always been very wary of using them, and as that paranoia increased I dropped the use of all bar one. I just couldn't see the net benefits of using them, and most certainly couldn't see any benefits for the carp. I have found some evidence of them doing harm, but nothing to support the fact that they do any good. Basically, the only nut I use now is the tiger nut. A little while ago I was talking about using baits that carp will accept readily as food, and in this respect tiger nuts are something of a conundrum. It is fair to say that in terms of nutritional value they are of little use to the carp, so why are they such a good bait? I have no definitive answer to that question, but I suspect it's a little like kids and sweets. They simply like the taste and texture of the nuts. One of the main drawbacks is that they can sometimes become part of a never-ending baiting cycle. The carp gorge themselves on them, barely pausing to chew them. They go off to rest up and digest their meal and then excrete whole and partially digested nuts onto the lake bed. Along comes another group of fish that eats them, and the whole cycle is repeated once again. They are left feeling that they have had a good meal, but in reality have got very little out of it. The excessive use of tiger nuts means the carp lose condition and rarely gain any weight. If you are going to pre-bait and fish with them, then please use as little as possible and always prepare them properly.

Natural baits are yet another addition to the carp angler's armoury. By

Bait is just one part of the carp fishing jigsaw puzzle.

naturals I mean maggots, caster, worms and bloodworm. Of all the baits at our disposal, these will mimic best the food that the carp feed on every day. The carp angler could therefore be forgiven for thinking that these are the best baits to use. Unfortunately this is not always the case. Apart from worms, which of course can be collected free from our own back gardens, the others cost a fair bit of money and this may restrict their long-term use. The other downside is that everything else that swims in our lakes and rivers also loves them. I have found that winter is the best time to use these baits in any quantity. That said, there is little doubt that in a stalking situation they are the best available.

What I have tried to do here is to give you my overall thoughts on bait. There are obviously some omissions here but, as I said, I will only talk about the baits that I have used. To do otherwise would be pure speculation on my part. As stated, boilies and pellets are my preferences but they are by no means the only choices. I have offered some cheaper options and I hope that they may help. Bait is just one part of the carp fishing jigsaw puzzle. Good bait helps, but it still needs to be applied correctly in the right areas. One thing I have found for certain is that there is nothing to beat quality and carp know a top-quality bait when they see one! Now, I want to take a closer look at these individual baits and see what they are all about.

Boilies

Shelf-life Versus Freezer Baits

On the face of it, there may seem to be little difference between ready-mades and freezer baits. After all, aren't they both just little round balls of bait? Well, yes they are, but it is what they are made of and their nutritional value that make the difference. As I explained earlier in this chapter, ready-made, shelf-life boilies are the carp fishing equivalent of a fast-food burger joint. Made from ingredients that are generally considered less nutritious than their frozen counterparts, they rely on a low-level preservative to keep them from rotting on the tackle shop shelves. But ensuring their longevity means that they can be stored at home or on the bank for indefinite lengths of time, so their most alluring feature is convenience. Walk into the tackle shop, buy a bag of what takes your fancy, and use them whenever they are required. Simple! Well yes, but you will need to be aware of a couple of points. In my experience this kind of boilie is not best suited to long-term bait application. Their lack of nutritional content will soon alert the carp to the fact that they are not doing them very much good and, relying as these boilies do on liquid attractors, it does not take the carp long to associate their particular smell with danger, and start to avoid areas baited with them. I *have* used them in the past to good effect, but only when I have been doing one-off visits to a water or just fishing short sessions. My advice, if you are going to use a shelf-life bait, is to pick one of the classic flavours such as tutti-frutti, pineapple or strawberry and you will not go too far wrong.

Convenience is the key word here and they really come into their own when considering a lengthy session or a trip abroad. The fact that they don't go off means that you can concentrate on the other important aspects of catching carp. In saying that, there is simply no substitute for quality.

In most cases freezer baits will be of a higher quality, and this means that they will be more nutritious. This kind of bait is ideally suited to anglers who are fishing the same venue all the time, be that a relatively easy water or one of the tougher low-stocked venues. These baits are

| Ready-made boilies have a big part to play… | …but freezer baits are ideal for long-term use. |

designed specifically to represent a long-term food source. By choosing a particular type of bait and sticking with it, the angler will get the carp accustomed to finding it and they will continue to eat it. The leading bait company I use has spent many tedious years perfecting the correct balance in their freezer baits so that the carp can get the most from them. Vitamins, minerals and usable proteins are just part of that process. One thing is for sure; the carp that eat this bait have achieved incredible weight gains and continue to be caught on them time and time again. And if that does not highlight the effectiveness of these baits, then let's take a quick look at how other species have benefited from their introduction to the water. At the time of writing, the records for bream, tench and chub are all held by carp anglers – proof enough to show how much everything is thriving because of its introduction.

The process of removing moisture and adding preservatives to shelf-life boilies simply doesn't allow for this level of perfection. The only downside of using a bait that is frozen, is that it will need to be managed correctly when out of the freezer. The active nature of the ingredients means that they have a tendency to go off, especially in warm weather. The trick here is keeping them fresh enough to ensure that they are doing what you want them to do. Not to worry though, as help is at hand.

The heat of the summer has the most dramatic effect on freezer baits.

So how can you tell when a bait is starting to go off or is, in fact, too rancid to use? Well, if they have gone too far, believe me you will know all about it. If you have never smelt a rotten boilie then you are in for a surprise. If you get it on your hands it takes an absolute age to get it off, and in all probability your partner won't let you anywhere near the house during that time! Normally, you can tell when boilies are going off when you detect a slight winy or vinegary smell. At this stage of the game they are destined for the bin because the point of recovery has passed. The first signs are normally the boilie appearing to sweat then a white, dusty coating begins to form on the outside. This is caused by moisture forcing the sugars out from the bait's proteins. These tend to colonise the surface of the bait, but when boilies in this state are broken open they look perfectly normal inside. Some anglers will use baits in this condition – indeed I have been tempted to do so myself in the past. However, your results will suffer if you do. No one will ever convince me that fresh is not the best.

When considering the longevity of your bait on the bank, moisture is public enemy number one. For the short-session angler – and by that I mean anything up to twenty-four hours – this will not be a problem. It is very likely that the first introduction of bait will be the only one, therefore it will be fresh. But beyond this timescale a little thought must be given to bait storage on the bank.

Preparation and Storage

I will now take a look at the methods of bait preparation and storage that have been successful for me. First of all, bait preparation for a 2–3 day session, and then for longer trips and travelling abroad.

For the shorter sessions the first thing I do is to take a couple of kilos of boilies from the freezer. These are then placed in an air-dry bag and I attempt to shake as much of the ice off them as possible. Once this has been achieved I leave them in the bag, hanging in the sun. The purpose of this is to get rid of the surface moisture; I am not trying to dry the bait out completely. This normally takes just a couple of hours. When I am happy that the surface moisture has gone, I fill a bait bucket one-third

An ideal way of keeping the boilies fresh.

full of pellets. Into these I pour my boilies. I give the bucket a good shake up to spread the pellets around and then I am ready to fish. The pellets will act as a desiccate, and by that I mean they will remove a lot of the remaining moisture from the bait. Prepared as I have described, the boilies will last several weeks, but keep checking them just to be on the safe side. A couple more tips before we move on. Never transport your freezer baits around in a plastic bag. This will only encourage the bait to sweat, thus increasing the moisture level and hastening their deterioration. I have found that a bucket is the best mode of transport. Also, ensure that you leave the lid of the bucket off as much as possible to allow the air to circulate. It goes without saying that should it rain, you must cover the boilies immediately – and don't leave them uncovered overnight because moisture will gather on them. All it takes is a little T.L.C.

The number of carp anglers travelling abroad is increasing on a daily basis. Many of the destinations have bait storage facilities, so you will not have too many problems keeping your bait fresh, but just as many don't. I have had the horrible experience of my bait going off during a long trip and, with nowhere to replace it, the whole journey can be a failure. Through bitter experience I have come to the following conclusions. Hopefully, we are never going to spend more than twenty-four hours travelling. For that reason I prepare my initial bait in exactly the same way as I do for a 2–3 day session in the UK. In all likelihood it will last more than a day or two. The last two bits of kit I pack into the car before I set off will be a bucket of pellets, and finally the boilies I retrieve from the freezer. These I store in a cold box or purpose-made cool bag. At least I will know that my bait is still, at worst, partially frozen on my arrival.

Once I have sorted myself out and am actually fishing, I turn my attention to the fresh bait. When dealing with large quantities of boilies, I normally carry a couple of unused carp sacks. It is into these that I place the fresh bait and they are then hung in a tree. If this is not possible, then I spread the boilies out on the ground on top of the sacks. Wherever I store them, I try to avoid direct sunlight for any length of time. I can't quite put my finger on the reason why, but this tends to dry them out too quickly and detracts from their effectiveness. Every couple of hours or so I move the boilies around in (or on) the sacks. This ensures that they dry out evenly. However, if you follow this procedure, never leave the boilies out overnight, whether hanging up or on the ground. Once again, we are trying to stop them being affected by more moisture. After a couple of days you can them store them in with the extra pellets that

Air-drying boilies.

you brought with you. And there you have it, bait to last you for a very long session indeed.

I am well aware that some anglers believe that this air-drying process will take something away from the bait. I must admit that I have had my reservations in the past. If I am not entirely happy with the end result, then I will attempt to re-hydrate them. Thankfully, most baits come with a dip that will enhance them to some degree. I normally carry with me several pots of this dip, which I pour over the air-dried baits, giving them an added boost. You will be surprised how quickly this liquid is soaked up, and to all intents and purposes you have a normal bait once again. But please ensure that, when you do this, you only

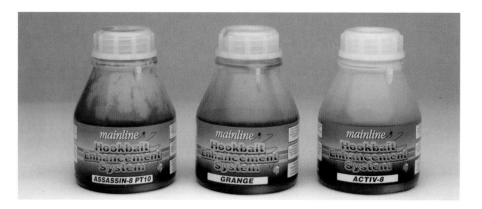

Dips also help to
re-hydrate the boilies.

re-hydrate enough bait for immediate use. The added moisture may facilitate decay if you do too many at once. Bait costs a lot of money, so in an effort not to waste it we must look after our bait and, by keeping it in good condition, we will get the best from it.

Rolling Your Own

For many years this was the only way that carp anglers could ensure a ready supply of boilies. Now, while the process of making your own bait may be classed as tedious, at the very least it allows you to have total control of the ingredients that your bait contains. Also, when you have created something of your own design, there is a massive sense of achievement when you catch a fish on it.

There is, of course, a massive downside to cooking up bait at home, and that will be the response of your wife or girlfriend. Some of the ingredients, not to put too fine a point on it, stink! The boiling process only compounds this further, and divorce proceedings have been hastened because of this. Be warned! Although it is a long time since I rolled my own boilies, there was a time when I tried to involve my wife in this, and for a while she went along with it. I am sure, though, that she breathed a huge sigh of relief once I started to use ready-rolled freezer baits – and so did the neighbours!

Most bait companies provide all the dry ingredients used in boilie manufacture and this is called the base mix. Along with the dry ingredients will come the liquid attractors. These will be added at the mixing stage and will help to make the bait even more effective. These ingredients will come with recommended recipes and levels for the attractors. My advice would be to follow these to the letter. After all, the company wants you to be as successful as possible with their bait and they are hardly likely to give you the wrong information.

To turn all the dry ingredients into a paste from which the boilies will be formed you are going to need eggs. Not only do the eggs bind everything together but, when boiled, the egg content helps to form a skin on the finished boilie. This holds in the attractors for longer periods, and makes the bait impervious to the attentions of smaller fish. A word of advice here – always ensure that the eggs you use are fresh. You may not think it possible, but the carp can definitely tell the difference.

Rolling your own bait can be a bit of a chore, but it really is very simple. What follows is a step-by-step guide and this will ensure that you end up with the perfect boilie.

The base mix.

Liquid attractors help to make the bait even more attractive.

All the equipment you will need.

Equipment You Will Need

The dry and liquid ingredients.

A mixing bowl and an implement with which to stir the ingredients.

A measuring device so that you can measure the ingredients accurately.

A saucepan large enough to hold the water necessary for boiling, and a deep-frying basket.

A clock to get the boiling times right.

A Rollerball type-rolling table.

Step by Step Process

1. Break the recommended number of eggs into the mixing bowl. Add the suggested amounts of additives and flavours and mix them together with a fork.

2. Carefully add the dry mix until you have a firm, workable paste (not dissimilar to the dough a bread-maker uses). As this dough thickens you will need to use your hands. A tip here is to use some of the dry mix on your hands to avoid it sticking. As eggs often vary in size, there is no need to weigh out a pound of dry mix. Simply keep adding it until the right consistency is achieved.

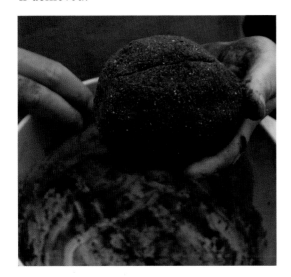

3. Roll the paste into sausages of the required diameter. This task is made much easier with the use of a bait gun or the reverse side of the rolling table. The size of the sausages will depend on the size of boilies you are aiming to produce.

4. Using the rolling table, start to roll the bait into balls.

5. The rolled paste balls should now be placed into the deep-fry basket, a few at a time. Don't try to do too many at once, and ensure that the water is boiling well before you place them in the saucepan.

6. Once the recommended boiling time has been reached, remove the bait from the saucepan and place the baits on a towel until they are thoroughly dry. This will probably take at least two hours.

7. Once the baits are dry they are ready to be frozen. Dedicated freezer bags can be bought from any supermarket, and the bait can be placed and stored in these.

Once you have become proficient at bait-making, you may wish to start adding your own ingredients or even creating your own bait. This trial and error can be very rewarding, but please ask the advice of the manufacturer as this will save a great deal of heartache. Believe me, I know!

Pellets

I mentioned the fact that I have a great love of pellets earlier in this chapter. That love was born from the way in which carp react to them. In the nineteen-seventies, trout pellets were used to form a paste, which was then used as a hook bait. With the advent of the boilie their use was forgotten, or at least limited, for a time. In the mid nineteen-nineties they made a massive resurgence; one that continues to this day, with good cause. I have not fished any water where I have felt their use has hindered me from catching fish in any way. From the easiest of venues to some of the hardest waters in the world, they have been instrumental in most of my successes.

Once again, the choice that is available to us is almost endless. Every bait company seems to produce a pellet of some description. To list all that are available would take a book in itself, so once again I think it best if I discuss those that I am familiar with. As I said, the mid nineteen-nineties saw their use become widespread, but many people had concerns about the high oil content of the pellets and the harm that this may do to the fish. A good friend of mine, who is a government scientist, was at the heart of this investigation. It was his findings that led me to believe that I should be using pellets that are low in oil. Trout pellets, as

There is a vast choice of pellets available today.

the name suggests, were used in the rearing of trout. However, once released into commercial trout fisheries, the trout in all probability would never eat another pellet, so the effects of long-term use were unknown. Carp, on the other hand, if fed large amounts of oily pellets year in and year out, can become out of condition and, in extreme cases, die. Slowly, over the course of time, bait manufacturers switched on to this and most pellets that are produced today are safe.

For some time, I had used trout pellets as they came out of the bag. As always though, I was looking to give myself an added advantage. What I started doing was to use the flavours and attractors from my boilies to over-spray the pellets. The new low-oil pellets soaked up a lot more of this liquid and made them ideal for the task. Not only was I baiting-up with something that I knew would catch carp; I was also introducing the attractors of the boilies I was using. This made baiting-up so much less expensive.

As time moved on, the bait company that I am involved with started to bring out pellets that complemented their boilies. They made a much better job of this than I did and, at a stroke, my life became much easier. So much so in fact, that they now form the mainstay of any baiting campaign and fishing venture that I undertake.

Pellets that carry the same food signals as my boilies – lovely!

Many of today's experienced carp anglers believe that using different sized pellets helps when tackling cautious and wary carp. The thought behind this is that, since they will be picking up varying sizes of free offerings, this will make it difficult for the carp to isolate the hook bait. I won't argue with that stance, but the only other pellet that I use today is a red fish betaine pellet. The fact that these pellets are red may have some bearing, but I use them mainly to add extra attraction to the baited area. The low-oil pellets that I now use tend to break down a lot more quickly and thoroughly than their high-oil counterparts. Size, in this case, is therefore irrelevant. Pellets can be purchased in a whole host of sizes, from tiny, almost dust-like particles to absolute gob-stoppers of an inch diameter and beyond. It's just a case of finding a size or combination to suit your needs.

As we have already discussed, pellets were used many years ago to form paste baits, and even today the flexibility of this bait still comes to the fore. The paste was formed by pouring hot water on the pellets and then working them into a dough. The same can be done today to form groundbaits and method mixes. They also make great PVA bag ingredients. Their inherent dryness will not damage the PVA and they also help to remove any moisture from other ingredients you may wish to use in a bag mix.

All these benefits mean that pellets are probably the most flexible bait on offer today. Made mainly from fishmeal, they provide the carp with a good nutritional food source and because of that they will go on working for as long as we want them to.

Pellets will keep on working.

Hemp pellets give another dimension.

Particle Baits

Seeds

In the nineteen-seventies, Redmire pool in Herefordshire probably had the greatest and most innovative carp angling minds on its syndicate. The most famous of these was the legendary Rod Hutchinson. It was Rod who really brought seed baits to the fore and the rest, as they say, is history. From that day to this they have been responsible for countless thousands of carp captures, and for my part, I believe they always will. When the boilie and hair rig revolution started in the early nineteen-eighties, these seeds lost something of their popularity. However, as time passed and pressure grew, carp anglers began once again to look for viable alternatives and seeds seemed to fit the bill quite nicely.

Seeds tend to be fished as a groundbait, or rather a background feed, when fishing other kinds of bait. The fact that carp will search around for every last bit ensures that the fish will stay in your swim for longer and, the longer they stay and are feeding, the more likely they are to encounter the hook bait.

I have rarely seen seeds being used as the actual hook bait. In the main, I think this is because they are so difficult to mount on the hair. In the

vast majority of situations anglers will be using bigger baits such as boilies on the hook. And herein lies one of the main problems with seed baits. The carp can very often get so preoccupied with finding and eating every single last seed, that they ignore the larger food items. For this very reason I never use vast quantities of seeds when I am fishing, preferring to introduce them in equal quantities with the boilies and pellets. One of the best ways to avoid carp ignoring the hook bait is to introduce a combination of seeds. The first time I became aware of this was with the hemp and groats mix. Although the seeds were of similar size, this gave the carp another option to search out, and in doing so they became more catchable. These multi-seed mixes have now become very popular, and rightly so. Pigeon conditioner and Parti-Blend being the best I have come across.

Seeds seem to be very instantaneous baits, and need little in the way of pre-baiting for them to work. Even carp that have never seen angler's baits (yes, there are still waters around like that) accept them readily. It is not only the attractors that seeds leak out into the water that bring carp into your swim. Seeds are very small, and this in turn attracts the

Parti-Blend: a great multi-seed mix.

Corn has stood the test of time.

attention of other, smaller species. The feeding activity of these smaller fish undoubtedly attracts the attention of the carp and they eventually bully out the other fish, ensuring that they get the lion's share of the meal. However, a word of caution here. Because the smaller fish find the seeds just as attractive as the carp do, there is every likelihood that they will eat a great deal of them before the carp arrive. Therefore, I have always found it best to top up the areas once or twice a day. First, this keeps the small fish feeding in the swim and second, it ensures that the carp will have a ready supply of bait once they arrive on the scene.

I have been fishing for carp on and off for the past twenty-five years, and over that time I have used many seed-type baits. These include hemp, groats, tares, red dari seeds, maize, corn, black-eyed peas, maples and chickpeas. Of these, only hemp, maize, corn and several multi-seed mixes have lasted the test of time. As with all aspects of carp fishing, confidence is the key here and these I will use with no worries at any time.

With the exception of corn, which can be bought ready cooked in tins or in freezer bags, the rest will need some kind of preparation before being put in the water. First, many seeds can be very dangerous to carp if they are fished in their natural state. Second, the process of soaking and boiling helps to release the baits' natural oils and sugars, making them far more digestible. In discussing preparation I will use hemp as an example, but this process is just as good with all the other baits I have mentioned. Please remember that seeds will swell by up to a third of their original size during this process.

Preparing Hemp

Half-fill a large bucket with hemp.

Fill the bucket with water until the level is just below the top of the bucket. It is preferable to use the water from the lake you are fishing, but this is not always possible.

Leave this to soak overnight.

Fill a saucepan with the soaked hemp and water and bring to the boil for twenty minutes. Repeat this process until all the seeds have been boiled.

You will notice that the seeds begin to spit. Not all of them will do this, but the vast majority will.

At this stage, the bait is ready for use. If you do not intend to use all the hemp immediately, then some of it can be frozen.

I prefer to use my hemp as fresh as possible, but there are others who like it when the seeds have started to ferment slightly. There are others who like to flavour their seeds. While I have no experience of doing this myself, it is a tactic worth considering. Confidence and experience will let you know what is best for you.

Nuts

I mentioned at the start of this chapter that I am not a great lover of nuts in any form. My suspicions have been confirmed over the years by looking at carp that have been exposed to mass introductions of this kind of bait. While they offer very little in the way of nutritional value for the carp, there can be no doubt that they find them irresistible at times. Texture and taste are the only reasons that I can think of for them to continually eat them.

Nuts are incredible carp-catchers.

The fact that they are incredible carp-catchers has often led me to use too many in the past. It's a battle of conscience at times. They catch lots of carp, and that is what we are trying to achieve. But the downside is that the carp will eventually lose condition and drop down in weight. If I am going to use nuts, a situation that occurs less and less these days, I will fish with the minimum amount. Please bear this in mind if you are intending to use them. Just because they fall into the category of particle baits doesn't mean that they have to be introduced by the bucket load!

I will run through the nuts that have used. There are more out there but, again, it would be wrong of me to speculate and talk about baits that I have no knowledge of.

Peanuts

I used these many, many years ago, but soon became aware of the danger they pose to carp. Not to put too fine a point on it, I will not use them now because they are harmful to carp. The most obvious place to buy them is a pet food shop. However, peanuts that are of bird food grade are carcinogenic. All types of peanuts, even the human grade ones, are very high in fat and this will cause a vitamin E deficiency in carp. They have thankfully been banned on the vast majority of waters, and rightly so.

Tiger Nuts

These are probably the most widely used nuts today. Their influence on carp fishing has been, and continues to be, massive. You may well have heard stories that tiger nuts can cause internal damage to fish. I haven't experienced anything to support that and totally disagree. I have seen carp excrete large amounts of broken swan mussel shells (swan mussels form a large part of their natural diet) onto the unhooking mat. Some of these pieces have been as large as 50-pence coins, with edges as sharp as razors. If these are not causing damage, then I don't think we have to worry too much about a tiger nut. However,

Tigers are probably the most widely used nut.

as mentioned earlier, problems can arise when carp become completely addicted to them. As the carp wolf them down, barely pausing to chew, the whole nuts tend to be excreted, and then eaten again by other carp. This will cause the carp difficulties because they are not getting a varied diet. If I seem to be labouring this point then I make no apology for that: used in excess tiger nuts can be dangerous.

Preparation is the key here. If prepared properly, tiger nuts not only become more digestible for the carp, they also release more of their natural sugars and attractors. And this is what the carp find so alluring. The process I will now outline is the same for all the kinds of nuts that I have used. Please remember that the nuts will swell up, sometimes to twice the size of their natural form.

Half-fill a large bucket with the tiger nuts.

Now fill the bucket with water to about an inch from the top.
Leave to soak for 48 hours.

Fill a saucepan with equal amounts of water and nuts and boil for 20–30 minutes. Continue this process until you have boiled the whole bucket load.

The tiger nuts will now be ready for use. Alternatively, you can bag them up and put them in the freezer for future use.

Tiger nuts will swell up during the boiling process.

I have used hazel nuts with varying degrees of success.

Carp find Brazil nuts hard to ignore.

As I said, tiger nuts have other functions apart from being used whole. Many of today's spod mixes, stick mixes and groundbaits contain tiger nuts in one form or another. Desiccated tiger nut is a great binder for groundbaits, and stiffens up spod mixes very nicely. The powder obviously carries the attractors of the whole nut, but since it is combined with other food sources it will not cause any problems. Chopped tigers are another great addition to these mixes. However, they will require the same preparation as the whole nut.

Hazel Nuts

I used these for some time back in the nineteen-eighties with varying degrees of success. Unfortunately, at their centre is a small air pocket and they are very likely to float. My only advice here is to ensure that, once they have been prepared, you only put into the lake the ones at the bottom of the bucket! One nice thing about these nuts is the colour of the water that you get once they are boiled. It turns a red, almost purple colour, and I have found this to be a marvellous substance to use when making up groundbaits and spod mixes. The cloud effect it sends up is awesome.

Brazil Nuts

The size of these large nuts tends to take them out of the range of what most anglers would refer to as a particle. I have had limited success with them, probably through not giving them enough of a chance. That said, many of my friends use them for a lot of their fishing. Of all the nuts I have used, these are probably the oiliest and once again the carp can find this difficult to ignore. Their large size also helps to foil the attempts of smaller species picking up the bait. The only downside (apart from being used in too large quantities), is that they do have a tendency to float. A useful tip here is to save any floaters for use as hook baits.

Size and Shape of Bait

So far I have used the boilie as my main example when discussing bait and I will continue along those lines in this section. With boilies being so popular, carp in the majority of our lakes have come to see them as a natural food source. The problem here is that they will, in many cases, also associate them with an element of danger. Frequently, whilst feeding on these little round balls, they will have witnessed one of their number bolting off, having made a mistake with the hook bait. Nevertheless, instinct will tell them that by feeding with caution they may well get a free meal. This instinctive process is made vastly easier for the carp by our own predictability. Travelling around the angling world, this is something I witness on far too many occasions. An angler turns up at the lake and casts out his marker float, then casts out his hook bait as near to that marker as he can. He then gets hold of the catapult and out go twenty or thirty large boilies. The same process is repeated with the other rods. If the bait is good enough, then in all likelihood the free bait will get

A very predictable baiting pattern.

eaten and the hook bait left alone. The angler will be blissfully unaware of this. Believe me, it happens a lot more than we think. The rods are reeled in twenty-four hours later, and the angler is left wondering why he hasn't caught a carp. Please forgive me if that sounds a little patronising; it is not intended to be. What I am trying to convey here is a situation that the carp are seeing over and over again. They become extremely adept at eating the free offerings and ignoring the hook bait. The best way to catch carp is to keep them guessing and whilst they are guessing, they become so much more catchable.

Size

I would guess that the most popular size of boilie used is 18 mm. Now, if the majority of anglers are using this size of bait then it all becomes a bit predictable. It has been written many times that, wherever possible, we should try to do things a little differently. If, for instance, you can see others using bigger baits, then using smaller baits will help to confuse the carp, as it is a situation that they may not have come across before. Of course, that can work the other way around, by using larger baits when small baits are popular, but in my experience the effect is less dramatic.

In an effort to cover all the options, I have taken to using as many different sized boilies as I can get hold of. My favourite combination is

of 10 mm, 14 mm and 18 mm. In this situation it is very hard for the carp to isolate and ignore the hook bait. Add some pellets to an area baited like this, and you now have four different sized baits for the carp to sort out. A bonus of this is that it gives you a far greater choice when it comes to selecting the size of your hook bait. (There are other ways of improving this situation, which I will come to shortly when I discuss the shape of the baits we use.)

Particles come naturally in different sizes. If these are the bait you intend to use, then by choosing multi-seed mixes or chopped and whole nuts you will be achieving the same goal. However, some

Wraysbury's Mallins, caught over a lot of different-sized baits.

Particles come in all different sizes.

Halved and quartered baits make the baited area more interesting.

Crumbed boilies keep the carp in the area longer.

particle baits are very difficult to present on the hair, so ensure that you use some larger items when baiting up. This will give you a varied choice of hook bait.

If you only introduce large items of bait, then it will not take long for the carp to clear them up. It would surprise a great many anglers just how much bait carp can eat, and how quickly they can clear an area. By using lots of different sized baits you are keeping the carp in your swim for longer. And the longer they stay there, the more likely you are to catch one.

(Notwithstanding what I have just said, when I am pre-baiting a lake just with boilies, I do so with the larger sizes only. In this instance I am trying to make the bait easy for the carp to find, not to confuse them in any way.)

Shape

The majority of boilies that you find on the tackle shop shelves will be round. I have absolutely no problem with this. By using different sized boilies I have never found that I am missing out on anything. Others however, have taken to making their bait into dumb-bell shapes, or even cubes. Confidence will once again play a huge part in their choice of bait shape and this is an avenue well worth exploring. Not having used these baits, it would be unfair of me to go into much detail, but I am sure they do help to confuse the carp.

What I do is break up my baits into halves or quarters and smaller. Not only is this introducing an untold number of different shapes of bait, it also allows more of the bait's flavour to leak out into the water – and that makes the baited area even more exciting for the carp. I very rarely fish these days without using chopped baits. Taking that a stage further, you can crumble up the boilies and in so doing add another dimension to the baited area. The obvious disadvantage here is that this kind of bait cannot be catapulted very far. These crumbs do, however, make an excellent addition to spod and bag mixes.

A point to note is that smaller boilies can be a little more expensive to buy, because their production is more labour-intensive. Therefore, I only use the larger boilies when I am breaking them up, saving the smaller ones to use just as they are.

Spod, Stick, Groundbait and Method Mixes

All three of these mixes are designed to get smaller items of bait accurately around the hook bait. Match anglers have been using groundbait very effectively as part of their fishing for years. It took some time, but carp anglers eventually switched on to this brilliant idea and this has spawned a whole host of other ideas and applications. Many of the ingredients used in the make-up of all these mixes will of course overlap. In fact, the potential list of ingredients would be almost limitless. Therefore, once again, I want to look at the baits that have been successful for me.

Spod Mixes

Before I look at the spod mixes that I use, it is worth mentioning that any bait can be put in a spod. Many anglers shy away from using boilies in their normal round form, because they very often get jammed in the spod and do not release. There is nothing more frustrating than reeling in the spod from a long way out, only to find it still full of bait. To avoid this happening with boilies, what I do is put a small amount of pellets into the spod at the same time as the boilies, trying to ensure they are evenly distributed. The pellets keep the boilies separate and stop them jamming in the spod, ensuring their release every time.

The dry spod mix ingredients.

There is, of course, a dedicated Spod Rocket, which is a much thinner tube. The boilies are simply loaded in and released once the spod hits the surface. This is fine if boilies are all you want in your swim. The downside is that I can get twice as many baits in a larger spod using the pellets.

The basic ingredients of the spod mix that I am currently using are desiccated nuts, hemp, and groats. This allows me a certain degree of flexibility. For instance, if I find that hemp is catching well on a certain water then I can simply add some more into the original mix. All that I need to do is add a similar amount of

Just add boiling water.

Pellets help to thicken up the mix.

Evaporated milk is an ideal additive.

Use your imagination…

boiling water to a bucket containing the dry mix, leaving it to soak overnight. If the mix is too stiff then I simply add a little more boiling water. On the other hand, if it is too runny then I can add some more dry mix or pellets. Once happy with the consistency, I can then add any other ingredients; perhaps some chopped tiger nuts, or maybe even a certain type of boilie. Our own imagination is all that limits us here. One thing's for sure, it is fun to experiment, and that is one of the joys of carp fishing.

Stick Mixes

The details of fishing with sticks are discussed further in Chapter 11. I have to admit that, as popular as this method is, I have very little experience of using it. Why that should be I am not sure, because it can be quite devastating. The tightly packed ingredients tend to explode when on the bottom of the lake, and form the most mouth-watering attraction in the immediate area of the hook bait. I will outline the mixes that I have used. These were not of my making, but were passed on by a good friend.

Dry Mix 1
Crushed hemp
Crushed tiger nuts
Salmon fry crumb
Crushed boilies
Small pellets
To this I add salmon oil, but only in the warmer months

Dry mix 2
Liquidised bread
Coleman's Fajita mix
Garlic salt

Perfect stick mix ingredients.

PVA-friendly liquids further enhance the mix.

Remember that a lot of bait companies now supply dips and additives that are PVA-friendly, and are an ideal addition to the mix. If you want to crumble up some boilies, why not include some of the accompanying dip? This will further enhance the stick mix. A couple of other good additions include hot chilli powder, Madras curry powder and soy sauce. There are plenty of other things to experiment with; just use your imagination. Here are some tips when using the stick method.

1. Keep the hook end of the stick for the very fine ingredients. Big pellets and chopped boilies go at the other end. This ensures that the hook point isn't masked by being impaled on one of the larger items.

2. Beware of over-oily mixes that are made up in advance of a session and are stored in a bucket – always test one in the margins to see that they are melting okay.

3. Use a plunger system against a flat, hard surface to create tight, compact sticks that break apart properly.

Groundbait and Method Mixes

Many of the ingredients in my stick mixes can be used in groundbaits, and once again it is only our imagination that limits us here. Of course, if you walk into the local tackle shop you will see a vast array of groundbait mixes. While I am sure that these are very good, they can also work out quite expensive. For that reason, and the fact that I believe they make better groundbait, I base my mixes on pellets. Not only do carp find them attractive, they also help bind the ingredients and hold things together when catapulting or using a groundbait sling. This is something to bear in mind when you make up your mixes. Some of the better additives I have used are hemp, corn, small boilies, dry pellets, tuna, chopped tiger nuts and groats. Don't forget the dips and glugs that bait companies supply as they can make groundbait so much more appealing. And this is how I make it up:

Half-fill a large bucket with your chosen pellets.

Pour boiling water over the pellets, but only enough to make the pellets fluff up a bit on the surface. Once this has been achieved, drain off the excess water.

Wait a few minutes for the pellets to cool down a little and test them. You are looking for a loose paste consistency.

Once you are happy that the pellets will bind, you can start to introduce your additives, both solid and liquid. Be careful not to put too much in, as this will make it hard for the damp pellets to bind it all together.

Some of my favourite groundbait and method ingredients.

For short-range work you can use this immediately, but when longer ranges are required I ball it up and leave the balls out to air-dry for a while. This will form a thin layer on the surface, which helps the balls of groundbait survive the rigours of being launched a long way. This is especially important when using the sling.

For method mixes I would not put so many of the larger items in. Although the groundbait ball will be put under stress from a catapult or sling, this will be further accentuated when cast out with a rod and line.

Natural Baits

We have discussed some of the particle baits that grow naturally in the wild but, however good these are, they are not things that carp will find and feed on in their normal environment. We do have at our disposal though some natural baits which, at the very least, mimic their everyday food – and some that are exactly that. This alone can sometimes elicit an immediate response. When stalking, this can prove invaluable, but these

Natural baits.

Red maggots are my favourite.

baits can still be utilised in normal angling. The main problem here is that everything else in the lakes and rivers loves them just as much as the carp do. There is a danger that these baits will be pecked at so much by smaller fish that they will come off the hair. In more extreme situations, you could have a sleepless night as bream and tench make the most of this appetising meal. All is not lost though. I am quite aware that when people go carp fishing that is the only thing they want to catch. But sometimes, when the carp are not really interested in feeding, we need something to get them in the mood. I call it 'inviting everything to the party'. By encouraging everything in the lake to feed on your baited area, carp will soon get the message and muscle in on the action.

I am going to discuss four of these natural baits, and how to get the best from them. Although there are other, more exotic baits, I have no experience with them and I cannot comment on their use with any authority.

Maggots

There is not an angler alive who hasn't heard of or, indeed, used maggots at some point or another. Outside of carp fishing, they must be the most widely used bait of all. Without doubt they are very, very attractive to carp. I much prefer the red maggots to the white ones. They imitate more accurately what the carp would feed on naturally, and therefore don't seem to generate too much suspicion on their part. Maggots are underused for carp for two main reasons. One, they are very expensive and this can limit their long-term use. Two, they are not very selective. I have found, however, that if I use a big bunch of them on the hair, it is too much of a mouthful for the smaller species, but carp will readily wolf them down.

Generally, I use them when spodding out other items of bait. By having them on my baited spots, I can get a lot more response from other fish and that, in turn, will attract carp to the area.

I always read about match anglers, and their efforts to keep maggots as fresh as they can. I have found the reverse to be true when targeting carp. After a day or two, maggots start to smell of ammonia. This is caused by the waste products they produce and seems to attract the carp more readily.

I have heard lots of anglers say that the reason why they don't use maggots is because they will crawl away from the baited area, or hide under stones and leaves. Believe me, once they are immersed in the cold water with no oxygen to breathe, they have far more to occupy them than finding a nice rock to rest up under! It's called survival, and they will not stray far from the hook bait. In any case, I have found that once the carp have discovered there are maggots on the menu, they will try to find every single one. This keeps them in the baited area for longer, and the longer they are there, and feeding, the more likely you are to hook one!

Casters

These crunchy little packets of bait are definitely my favourite natural bait. Carp find them simply irresistible, and apart from the fact that they taste good, I believe they like the crunchy effect when chewing them up. Again, they

Big bunches are often avoided by the smaller fish.

Casters are a devastating natural bait.

Chopped worms release more attractors into the water.

Frozen bloodworm.

are very expensive and unlike maggots they are not so durable on the hair. Small fish make mincemeat out of them in a short space of time. I tend to fish them these days in conjunction with maggots. In saying that, I have no worries using them in a stalking situation, where I can see what is happening to the hook bait. They don't stay fresh as long as maggots do, so require a bit more looking after. Once they go too dark, they will float.

Worms

Worms need little in the way of introduction as a fish attractor extraordinaire. I am no expert, but I believe they are packed full of all the attractors we will ever need to get fish feeding in the swim. They can be very expensive to buy from a tackle shop, but why bother? Most of us have access to a garden, and there you will find an almost inexhaustible supply. All it takes is a little hard work. In fact, in the time it will take you to drive to the shop you could have dug up a hundred or so. I rarely use them whole because their lively wriggling sometimes allows them to mask the hook point. I prefer to spend a few minutes chopping them up with a pair of scissors. This not only makes the wriggly little fellows go a bit further but, more importantly, releases the wonderful fish-attracting juices into the water.

Bloodworm

Although these have been used in angling for many years, it has only been in recent times that they have been used to any great extent in carp fishing. I have little faith in products that say they contain bloodworm, so I use the creatures as they come. Not having a clue how they are harvested, I buy them frozen. Now, although these will be dead, they are still very attractive to carp. They make an excellent addition to spod and groundbait mixes.

Artificial Baits

Of all the modern-day developments in carp fishing I have to admit that this aspect is one that took me a long time to come to terms with. I simply could not understand why a carp would want to eat a little piece of plastic. For years, in not using them, I did not think I was missing out on a thing. I was catching plenty of carp and that's all that mattered. More and more though, articles and catch reports in the magazines and papers indicated that carp were getting caught everywhere on this intriguing invention. It was time for me to take a closer look. Being somewhat slow on the uptake, I still couldn't rationalise their use. I think

Artificials.

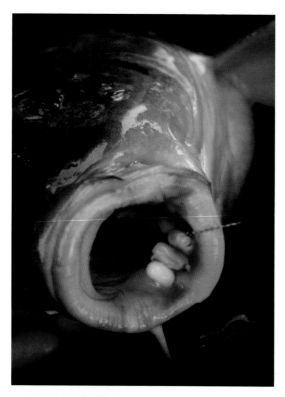

Plastic corn helped in the downfall of this carp.

the turning point may have come when the British record was caught on some plastic corn. If a carp which is under that much pressure could succumb to it, then I simply had to take it more seriously.

There are an awful lot of good carp baits out there, but many of them are not very resistant to the attentions of smaller fish, or to being submerged in water for long periods. There is nothing worse than sitting worrying if you still have a bait on the hook or hair. The first kind of plastic bait, as far as I know, was the imitation corn, and corn is a classical example of the kind of bait I am talking about here. It's very soft, and the only way to know if the bait is still on is by constantly re-casting – which is not an ideal situation when you are trying not to frighten off the carp. And talking of casting, if we intend to fish at long range there is every danger of the hook bait flying off the hair when we do so. Plastic hook baits stay where we put them!

As I said, I was reluctant to use artificial baits because I didn't understand how a carp would think it was actually something to eat. But, when you think about that, a carp can only tell if something is edible by picking it up in its mouth. It has no hands to test the thing with! If a carp picks up a bait, and the rig is efficient, then we should hook it. Even so, for some time I would only use artificial baits when I was fishing over a quantity of bait. But, as time has moved on, I have caught using just a single plastic hook bait. Strange, but true.

For a while, I was convinced that, while they worked, plastic baits did so because they didn't smell of anything and this meant that there were no danger signals to alert the carp. Yet again I was proved wrong. Plastic baits can be flavoured, and these work just as well. Simply soak them in the dip of your choice for a few days and they are good to go.

The artificial baits available today mimic just about every kind of bait you care to mention. Corn we have already talked about, but what of the natural baits I spoke of earlier? Plastic maggots, casters, hemp and maize, not forgetting the more exotic baits such as prawns and mussels, are all out there. There are even plastic dog biscuits available to use for surface fishing. In their natural form, these are good carp baits, but they won't last long in the water. The plastic baits have relieved us of this worry. They come in pop-up or normal sinking varieties, so the choices of presentation are still there. Nice! Taking this one stage further, you will now find on your tackle shop shelves 'night glow' versions. As strange as it seems, these baits catch carp, and lots of them!

A carp falls to plastic maggots.

Presenting Hook Baits

Much of my fishing emphasis centres on the bait that I am using. I would go as far as to say that, coupled with a sharp hook, bait is the most important factor for me. For many, many years I believed that I had to have a hook bait that mirrored, exactly, the free offerings I was using. This philosophy stood me in good stead for a long time, and is a tactic I still use today. However, as with all aspects of carp fishing, things have moved on.

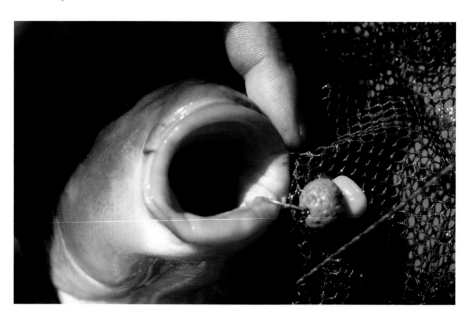

A perfectly presented hook bait.

The inventive minds of some very clever anglers have taken thinking about hook baits way beyond this simple concept. As I said, for many years I was quite happy simply to take a bait from the free offerings bag, and put it on the hair. But because carp became more wary as the pressure on them increased, anglers started to look for ways to add a little buoyancy to their hook baits. Initially, this was done to negate the weight of the hook, something that could possibly alert the carp to the fact that something was not as it should be. I am not familiar with the precise history of popped-up hook baits, but one thing is for sure – on their day they can be quite devastating. Having a hook bait 2 or 3 inches above the bottom, and thus above the free offerings we have introduced, may appear to be totally at variance with the idea of making the hook bait blend in with the loose feed, but pop-ups work.

Taking that thought a stage further, anglers are now making the hook bait look completely different from anything else they may have introduced. The thinking behind this is that it will be the first thing the fish will see and hopefully it will take that before anything else. This raises the subject of bait colour. There has been much speculation about what carp can and cannot see. While I agree that carp use all their senses to find food, I don't agree that sight is the main one. I keep asking myself, how the hell does a blind carp (and there are plenty of them) find its food? And what about night-time? It pays to keep an open mind on this subject. Maybe it is enough to know that carp can be caught on bright pink or yellow baits. Indeed, I know many anglers who fish with nothing else.

While I dealt with the size and shape of free offerings earlier in this chapter, the size and shape of the hook bait itself is another area that rewards investigation. There is no doubt in my mind that it is relatively easy for a carp to pick up and eject a 14 mm boilie. The advances in rig design have helped to overcome this problem to some extent, but what I want is something that the carp will find difficult to deal with. Larger baits are the obvious answer, and stepping up to a bigger boilie will help. Double and even triple baits will make it even harder for the fish to get away without being hooked. Cubed and dumb-bell shapes again increase this unmanageable effect. The problem we have to contend with here is that many anglers seem to be using smaller and smaller baits, which is compounding the problem, because a bigger hook bait will then stick out like a sore thumb. Thus, whatever size of hook bait I am using, I will be sure to introduce some baits of similar size when putting out my free offerings.

There has been much speculation about what carp can see.

By attaching any type of bait to the rig we will be affecting its natural movement. In other words, it will behave differently from all the loose feed. It stands to reason, therefore, that when we look at hook baits we have to give some thought to their actual presentation. Soft braided hooklinks will give the hook bait the greatest degree of movement, but even so I am not a big fan of them. My preference is for some kind of stiff boom section, coupled with a flexible section at the hook end of the hooklink. The stiff boom helps to keep the hook bait in the carp's mouth longer, and therefore increases the chances of the hook finding a hold. This effect can be achieved to some degree with the modern strippable braids, but by far the best way is to use a separate boom constructed of purpose-made thick nylon. Be mindful of how you want the hook bait to behave, and use something that will achieve that aim. We have the option of scaling down the tackle we are using, but we can only take that option so far because of the risk of leaving the fish towing tackle. Thus we tend to use quite crude gear, but I have never seen this as a hindrance at all. By giving some thought to our presentation, these problems can be overcome.

Pop-ups Versus Bottom Baits

When the use of pop-ups first became common knowledge, it still took a long time for many of us to believe that they would work. It is not until you actually use them that you see how effective they can be. I suspect that my reluctance to use them was born from the fact that I like to use lots of bait. If I intended the carp to feed hard on the bottom, then that is where I felt my hook bait should be. When I am using lots of particle baits such as hemp, then I am still inclined to use a bottom hook bait. However, when I am fishing over boilies and pellets, I now much prefer a pop-up. If the area allows, and I am not in danger of scaring the carp by introducing another line, then I will fish a bottom bait presentation as well. For some reason though, the pop-up seems to get the lion's share of the bites. Why this is so, I always find one of the most difficult questions to answer definitively. I suspect that confidence in what I am doing plays a large part in hook bait selection and all I can suggest is that you do the same. I have no doubt, however, that if you are using lots of bait in particle form then you should use a bottom bait on the hook. On the other hand, if you are scattering your bait, thus encouraging the carp to travel between mouthfuls, then it would be a pop-up for me every time.

Hook Bait Buoyancy

At the risk of sounding obvious, a pop-up needs to be as buoyant as possible, whilst a bottom bait requires no buoyancy aids at all. With the pop-up presentation it is possible to adjust how the bait rests on the bottom. With the addition of a little rig putty, we can make the pop-up sink very slowly or, by adding slightly more, make it sink quicker. Making it sink slowly offers the carp another problem. Whilst picking up the free offerings the carp will be using a certain amount of suction. When it attempts to pick up the hook bait, the normal amount of suction will send the hook bait shooting right to the back of its mouth. It is this simple action that encourages the carp to bolt, so unnaturally does the hook bait behave. The problem with a delicately balanced bait such as this is that, when carp are feeding actively in the swim, the hook bait can waft all over the place, and because it is tethered to a lead it can appear very unnatural. This can help the carp to isolate the hook bait and ignore it. What I try to achieve is a hook bait that sinks as slowly as

Double hook baits are difficult for the carp to pick up without being hooked.

It looks unnatural, but it works!

the free offerings. Then, at the very least, it will only waft up as much as the other baits in the swim.

This process of adjusting the buoyancy is often referred to as critically balancing the bait, and it is not used solely in conjunction with pop-ups. Bottom baits can also be made to sink more slowly and therefore behave more naturally. Indeed, many anglers use something called a 'wafter', which is a bait that will sit on the bottom, but the slightest disturbance will send it wafting around. This is a tactic I have never tried, but I have been assured that it works very well.

One other useful way of balancing baits is with lead wire. Instead of having putty or shot on the line as a counterweight, we can insert the lead wire into the bottom of a pop-up to achieve the buoyancy we require. The more you put in, obviously, the quicker it will sink. This is a very good way of turning pop-ups into balanced bottom baits. I always use a length that is a little longer than I think I will need. This allows me to trim off small pieces until the required sink rate has been achieved. Any excess sticking out of the bait is then pushed all the way in.

I use these for most of my pop-up fishing.

Making Pop-ups and Balanced Baits

To my mind, there is little or no point nowadays in preparing my own pop-up hook baits on a regular basis. Most bait manufacturers, including my supplier, now produce pop-ups to complement the range of boilies they make and I use these for 99 per cent of my fishing. To produce the 'wafters' I mentioned earlier, most of the anglers I know simply trim down one of the ready-made pop-ups to achieve the required buoyancy. That, in itself, should indicate how versatile these hook baits are.

However, there are still odd occasions when I like to make my own balanced baits and there are several ways to produce pop-ups and balanced baits, so I want to take a brief look at these before we move on.

To make cork ball pop-ups you will need to obtain a small amount of the dry mix of the boilies you are using. In the same way as I outlined in the earlier section on making your own bait, you have to produce a ball of paste. Because, for buoyant baits, you have to extend the normal recommended boiling time by a minute or two, I have always found it best to double the dose of liquid attractors. One other useful tip is to sieve the dry ingredients before forming the paste. This takes out the larger items in the mix and will add to the buoyancy and durability of your bait. Next, you will need a selection of cork balls. Obviously, the bigger they are the more buoyant they will be. I can give no advice as to how much paste to roll around these cork balls – you will have to experiment for yourself – but be conscious of the size of the boilie you want to end up with. In the same way, by using smaller cork balls we can produce balanced bottom baits.

There are other ways of making these sorts of hook baits. Most of the bait companies produce a mix specifically designed to make baits pop-up. These are simply added at the recommended rates to the dry mix. The paste is then made and the balls boiled as normal. I have not tried it myself, but cork dust can be added to the dry mix and this will have the same effect.

Preparing a cork ball pop-up.

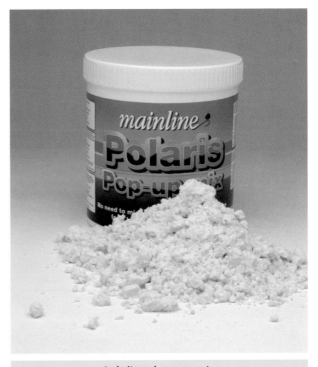

A dedicated pop-up mix.

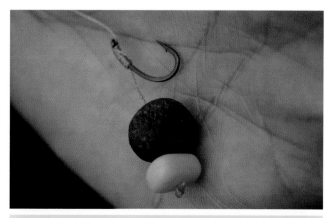

Pop-up corn is used to make a neat snowman presentation.

It helps to keep them guessing.

Multiple Hook Baits and Snowman Presentation

To my mind, one of the most difficult presentations for a carp to deal with is two or more hook baits together. This larger offering seems to be hard for the carp to eject efficiently because of its odd shape. With the ever-increasing trend towards smaller and smaller baits, this is worth trying: anything that the carp are unfamiliar with is likely to trick them. If I am using double hook baits, then I sometimes use PVA tape (see Chapter 11) to help me introduce

double free offerings. This gets the carp used to seeing and eating them. Taking this a stage further, we can incorporate three or more hook baits onto the hair. Although this tactic has worked, it is best to try to balance the whole set-up with a buoyant bait of some description. This will help the hook bait to go further into the carp's mouth once it has picked it up. Once in its mouth it becomes even harder to eject. Keeping the bait in the fish's mouth for longer gives the hook more time to find a hold.

One of my favourite multiple bait set-ups is commonly know as 'the snowman'. Basically, this is constructed by first putting a bottom bait on the hair, followed by a slightly smaller pop-up. If the bait produced is too buoyant you can use a lead wire insert in the bottom bait to get it to sit gently on the bottom. This presentation has much going for it. The buoyant nature of the bait helps the hook bait to enter the carp's mouth much further. If the carp you are fishing for are very rig-conscious, it helps that this hook bait will come to rest on top of the hook, thus disguising it further. The size and shape will make it difficult to eject. In recent years this set-up has accounted for the vast majority of my carp captures, and in most cases it is my primary form of presentation.

I make no apology for going into this subject of presentation in such detail. In today's pressured carp fishing environment, we need to have as many tricks up our sleeves as possible. Bait is a fundamental part of the carp fishing equation, but the carp are seeing good quality bait more or less on a daily basis. While I am sure that they eat most of what is introduced to a water, they also associate this with an element of danger. This means that they are not always feeding with as much gusto as we would like. When they are, you may hook them on the most basic of presentations, but most of the time we need to give this a great deal of thought. Pop-ups, multiple baits and balanced bottom baits are all ways in which we can keep the carp guessing. And while they are guessing, they are infinitely more catchable. The use of these different baits and presentations also allows us to fish over different kinds of lake beds with a great deal of confidence. A hook bait that sinks very slowly will come to rest gently on top of any debris and light bottom weed, minimising the likelihood of the hook point being masked.

You will doubtless have noticed that this chapter about baits is a very long one. It is so by necessity, because it is a huge subject. By the same token I feel that, apart from first finding your fish and using a sharp hook, bait is the next most important aspect of carp angling. The scope for your own experimentation here is massive, and I hope you enjoy learning more about the subject. Remember though, that quality is everything, and the carp will be the best judge of that!

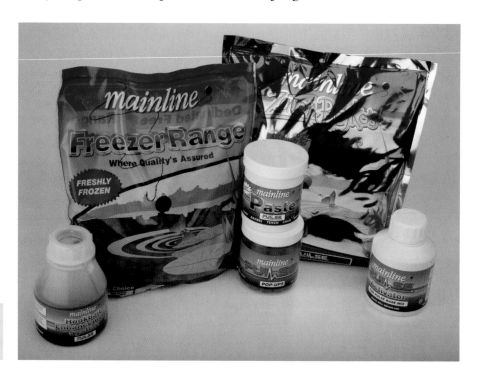

Quality is everything.

9 BAIT DELIVERY SYSTEMS

While there will be occasions when a single hook bait will be sufficient to get a take, that in itself is a tactic and not a baiting philosophy. By introducing free offerings we are first of all trying to attract the carp to the area, and then giving them enough confidence to pick up the hook bait. How much is introduced to the area is very much down to circumstances, individual judgement and confidence in that judgement. What is really important most of the time is accuracy. There is a theory that it is good to spread the bait far and wide, but I do not necessarily agree with this. I admit, however, that when fishing with boilies, I tend to spread them out a little more. This is because a carp that has to move between mouthfuls is much more catchable than one that is feeding in a static way. There is an inherent problem when using a mixture of different sized baits, as is the case when using particles and pellets. By firing them all out together, say from a catapult, some bits will travel further than others, and this is not what we want to achieve.

There are various methods of delivering bait, and different ones may be chosen depending on circumstances and what we are trying to achieve. While some of them are more or less self-explanatory, others, like spodding, will require more in-depth explanation. Let's have a look at what is available.

Baiting by hand in the margins.

By Hand

This is practically self-explanatory, but obviously has its limitations. This tactic can only really be employed when fishing in the near margins. There are a couple of pluses to this way of baiting-up though. First of all you can create the exact situation you want to achieve because the spot you want to bait is so near at hand. Baits of all sizes can be positioned with great accuracy. Second, if the water is fairly clear you will be able to see the results of your efforts. Once an angler is happy the boost in confidence is amazing.

Catapult

The catapult is probably one of the most widely used baiting-up tools, and manufacturers have made several models to meet various requirements. You see, a catapult is not just a catapult. You will need a different one for say, putting out balls of groundbait, as compared to one that is used to feed small particle baits. Thankfully, manufacturers have come to the rescue in this respect and you will find in their range a catapult to suit just about any bait. It will be up to you to select the one

The ever-popular catapult.

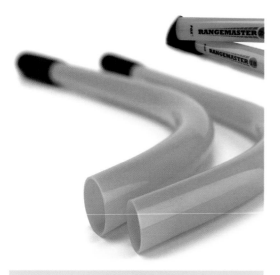

The ultimate tool for delivering boilies at range.

The boilie bum-bag keeps the bait readily to hand.

needed for the job. Ensure that you pack a supply of suitable spare elastics. These have a tendency to break, and it can be very frustrating if you cannot deliver the required amount of bait. If you are baiting-up with several different-sized items, it is best to introduce the smaller or lighter items first. This avoids the frustration of finding out that you cannot reach the chosen spot to which you have delivered the heavier items first.

Throwing Stick

This is probably the ultimate tool for delivering boilies at range. Its use, however, will take a little practice. My advice would be to get a bag of cheap ready-made boilies, and practise with them in a field. You may get some very funny looks from the local residents, but I can assure you that your time will not be wasted. It is not as expensive as wasting bait when you are actually fishing. Once the technique is mastered, it is possible to put out three or four boilies at a time, and this makes the whole process much less time-consuming. Because the stick will make the boilies spin, it is advisable to use baits that are rock hard, otherwise they will split when in flight. It also helps to moisten the inside of the stick with some lake water to aid the exit of the boilie(s) and increase the distance of travel.

When selecting a stick you must ensure that it will accommodate the size of boilie you intend to use. Small baits in a wide-bore throwing stick will rattle up the length of the tube and thus reduce the distances you can achieve.

Using a throwing stick is all about rhythm. If you haven't used one before, don't try to put the bait over the horizon on your first attempt. It's much the same as golf: get the technique right and the distances will come with practice.

One other useful tool to use is the boilie bum-bag. This allows you to have the bait readily at hand. Without the need to bend down and get the next handful of bait, you can maintain rhythm.

One of the downsides of the throwing stick is that the bait is very vulnerable to attack by the dreaded seagulls. I have watched anglers blindly carrying on with the throwing stick, thinking that the gulls are getting very little bait. This is a big mistake. I can assure you that, with their incredible eyesight and agility, they get every last one. Be warned!

The 'Method'

I wasn't quite sure where to include this particular tactic, but I think it best to put it here. After all, we are introducing a small package of bait into the water. This technique was first used in match fishing circles, the idea being to introduce bait frequently and therefore catch fish as quickly as possible. Very soon though, carp anglers adapted it for their own purposes. I will say at this point that I believe it is best suited to the more heavily stocked venues, since it relies heavily on the carp competing for food. On more lightly stocked venues, that competition rarely exists and this technique has not, in my experience, been any good.

The method feeders.

Ideal for the job.

This power grip method catapult is ideal for introducing extra groundbait balls to your chosen area.

Basically, this tactic requires the use of a method feeder, and there are plenty of these available to the carp angler nowadays. Around this frame is moulded a ball of stiff groundbait. The hook bait can be either fished on a short hooklink to keep it near the ball, or on an even shorter one so that the hook bait itself can be moulded into the method ball. The method is so effective because, much like PVA bags (see Chapter 11), you have a concentrated ball of bait for the carp to home in on. This, the carp will attack until the hook bait is taken. Then the whole process is repeated.

I have outlined the ingredients for method mixes in the previous chapter.

When method fishing, some consideration will have to be given to the rod that you are using. On small waters, where only a short cast is necessary, normal carp rods up to $2^{1}/_{2}$ lb test curve will suffice. But when distances above 30 or 40 yards are needed I would use a rod of at least 3 lb test curve. The feeder itself will probably weigh about 2 oz, and when it is fully laden with bait it will be around 5 oz, so you would be in danger of breaking a lighter

rod. I have a purpose-made 'method rod' and it will cast a well set-up feeder in excess of 90 yards.

Casting such heavy weights as these will also require you to use a leader of some description. This will avoid the main line breaking when you load up the rod to cast. The ideal leader in my experience is the tapered nylon type. These are 20 metres long and taper from 15 lb breaking strain up to 45 lb.

Lastly, it is necessary to consider the feeder itself. These are used on the line in much the same way as you would use an in-line lead. It is vital that, should your main line break, the fish is able to rid itself of the potentially dangerous feeder. The core of the feeder will have some weight added to it. This ensures that even if the carp have eaten most of the method mix, there is still enough weight to drive the hook home when the hook bait is picked up. Normally, the feeder will have three fins and it is these that secure the mix to the feeder.

Try not to overdo it on the bait front. What I do is use just enough so there are a couple of millimetres of mix covering the fins on the feeder. Above all, the safety of the rig must be uppermost in your mind: one, that you don't crack off when you cast and two, that the carp can rid itself of the feeder in the event of a breakage.

A fully loaded feeder ready to go.

My favourite bait delivery system.

Spodding

As we have seen, there are various ways of delivering bait to our intended fishing area. Most can be very effective, but they are limited in the range at which the bait can be delivered. Spodding is without doubt my favourite and most-used method of baiting-up. I find it incredibly satisfying to deliver a large amount of bait to a distant mark. It can, at times, seem like a laborious task, repeatedly loading the spod and launching it out into the lake, but for me that only adds to the challenge. I enjoy being as accurate as possible, and getting the spod to land with as little splash as I can. It is a skill that takes some practice but, in time and with the right equipment, unheard of distances can be achieved – and with surprising accuracy. So what is a spod and how do we get the best from it? Basically, a spod is a tube-like device that can be filled with bait and (using the right equipment) cast long distances. Many of the anglers to whom I have spoken on the bank feel that spodding is a relatively new introduction to our sport. However, the first time I became aware of it was way back in the early nineteen-eighties. On a very difficult and lightly stocked Home Counties lake, a group of friends employed this tactic, and in only a few short months they caught every fish in the lake. Because the spod itself was not then commercially available, they had to construct their own. In time though, one forward-thinking tackle company decided to make a spod available in the shops, and all of a sudden the method became very popular.

Unfortunately, a stigma that is sometimes attached to the use of a marker float is now being connected to spodding. The charge is that these techniques scare the carp. I will not argue against the fact that, in some extreme circumstances, they will do just that, but in the main their use is so widespread now that the carp associate them with the arrival of food. A couple of years ago, a fellow I know was using his spod on a very hard lake near to my home; a lake on which one or two fish a year is considered a good result. He was being watched by a couple of other anglers who were high up in a nearby tree. They were amazed to see one of the lake's largest residents, a carp well in

excess of 40 lb, taking the bait as it fell from the spod! He went on to get three takes over the following twenty-four hours!

Many anglers feel that, on these more challenging venues, they have to set subtle little traps for the carp (and, I must say, they do fairly well), and they state that they 'left the spod brigade to it'. However, on one notoriously difficult lake that I fished a couple of years ago, they left me to it and I ended up being the top rod for the season. Each to his own I guess – but the more arrows you have in your quiver the better, in my book. Anyway, enough of me blowing my own trumpet, let's take a rather more in-depth look as this subject.

As spodding became more and more popular, so the tackle industry started to produce equipment specially designed for the purpose.

I find spodding very satisfying.

Stronger rods helped to cast the heavy spods really long distances, and the spods themselves have gone through a very quick evolution. As with any other aspect of our sport, a little trial and error has led me to a set-up that is balanced and capable of getting bait to extreme distances. So where do we start?

Spod Rods

I see so many anglers struggling with rods that were never designed to cast a fully laden spod. If you do this, not only are you in danger of breaking the rod – you will also severely limit yourself so far as range is concerned. For some reason that I have never been able to fathom, purpose-built spod rods are very inexpensive, so price is hopefully not going to affect your decision to buy one. Bait is a massive part of the carp fishing equation, and if you cannot introduce bait effectively at range, then you are going to seriously limit the number of carp you will catch.

For years, I had been using a 12 ft, $4^1/_2$ lb test curve spod rod. It managed to deliver my bait to just about everywhere I wanted it to go, and never let me down. I then joined a syndicate water that required me to fish at otherwise unheard-of distances. This was testing my casting abilities to the extreme. I didn't have too many difficulties getting the hook bait in position, but baiting-up was proving a problem. Eventually, I managed to get my hands on a new $12^1/_2$ ft rod with a $4^1/_2$ lb test curve. The extra six inches have helped me to achieve the extra twenty or so yards I needed. A spod rod, however, is like any other rod in that what suits one person may not suit another. I would advise you to shop around a little and find out what is best for you. Ask anglers on the bank what they are using. Get as much feedback as you can before you make your decision. Believe me, when you find the right rod it will put yards on your casting.

One last thing before I move on. Spod rods look very robust, but this doesn't mean that they don't need looking after. By their nature, the baits that we spod out tend to cover the rod in all manner of bits and pieces, so it needs to be cleaned regularly. If the spigot section is covered in bait, this can easily weaken it and will eventually lead to a snapped rod.

The best spod rod I have ever used.

Spodding Reels

Spodding is a very labour-intensive exercise and, as much as it puts quite a lot of strain on the angler, it will also test tackle to the limit. Strain is particularly hard on the reel that you will be using, because of the repeated casting and retrieving. For my spodding, I use one of the modern big pit reels. Although that may seem to be a very heavy item to use repeatedly, it isn't a problem for me. In any case, even if it was, the pros definitely outweigh that single con. These larger reels seem so much more robust than their smaller brethren, and handle the rigours of repeatedly casting a heavy spod with ease. The line lay on these reels is also so much better. This definitely helps the line to leave the spool more easily, and will add dramatically to your casting range. Finally, one of the nicest aspects of these reels is that they have a very fast retrieval rate, which brings the spod in quickly. Retrieving the spod is one of the worst things about spodding, and anything that makes it a little easier is all right by me. As with the rod, make sure that the reel is cleaned and serviced regularly. All those little particles of bait can make a terrible mess of the gears if you are not careful.

I use a big, robust reel for my spodding.

Spodding Line

For many years I used nylon line for all my spodding. In an effort to increase my casting range, I have in the past gone down to line with a breaking strain as low as 4 lb. (The lower the diameter of the line, the further I could cast.) This, of course, was used in conjunction with a shock leader of much heavier breaking strain. As I wasn't catching carp on this light line I was able to get away with it. But while this suited for 95 per cent

14 lb braid and a 30 lb braided shock leader.

Imagine the damage that braid could do to your finger.

of my fishing it simply would not do for extreme range. You see, even with a thick nylon shock leader there is some stretch, and it was this stretch that I felt was hindering me from compressing the powerful rod. Compressing the rod fully is a sure-fire way of getting the maximum distance. To overcome this, I graduated to a braided shock leader and for a while this seemed to be okay. The problem was the lack of durability of the light nylon and I was forever replacing it.

I then started to use a 30 lb braid straight through, which meant I no longer had to use a shock leader of any kind. Now, although the 30 lb braid was relatively thin for its breaking strain, it did cut down my distance since it was still too thick, and prone to being caught by cross-winds, so I had to start looking for another answer. Eventually I found what I was looking for, in a very low diameter 14 lb braid that I used in conjunction with a 30 lb braided shock leader. That is the line that I use today. It is so fine and soft, I can't even hear it going through the rod rings. This lack of friction means that the spod sails out, giving me those extra yards.

Finally on line, a repeated word of warning. Thick nylon leaders are not too harsh on your casting finger, and you may well get away without protecting it. Braid, however, is a completely different animal and any small mistakes on your part may well result in your index finger looking like finely minced meat! The first thing to do is ensure that the clutch on your reel is screwed down as tight as it will go. This avoids any slippage. Second, get yourself a finger-stall or, more to my liking, a golf glove. Even if you have no slippage from the reel, in prolonged spodding the braid will do some damage to your finger.

The Spod

For a long time anglers used to construct their own spods, mainly from old washing-up bottles and similar things. They certainly did the trick at short distances, but were terribly ungainly at range. As the tackle industry took more and more interest in this method, things began to improve. The first commercially produced spod I saw was a fantastic revelation, but had one major drawback: if you wanted to use, shall we say, a more stodgy spod mix, it was a devil of a job to get it to drop out of the spod. A stodgy mix would cling to the inside of the spod and, under the compression of a powerful rod, it would compact even more and this was making the problem even worse. Some bright spark eventually brought out a spod with holes in it and the impact of the spod hitting the surface forced water through the holes, aiding the release of the bait. Very handy! Then the holes got bigger. Unfortunately, this meant that small items fell out and maggots could sense an easy route to freedom. Couple that with a bit of general spod spill, and it all meant that less bait was being delivered to the requisite spot. Then, as with most clever inventions, spods evolved that went a long way to solving these problems. The model that I use these days has several ingenious little touches. To help avoid excessive bait loss through the holes, I am able to insert a unique blanking cylinder. Maggots can no longer escape, and I can leave a couple of holes at the top of the spod to allow water to be forced in, which enables the bait to be released. These spods also come with interchangeable nose cones, and this ensures I can see the spod at range in any light conditions. Most spods these days come with a clip that you simply attach to the end of the main line via a swivel. This is a great help if you want to change the kind of spod you are using, since it saves cutting one off and tying on another.

The spod.

The unique blanking cylinder.

Of course, we may not always want to bait up with a dedicated spod mix – there will be times when we will only want boilies in and around the hook bait. Enter the boilie rocket. Basically, this is a slimmer version of the normal spod, which allows the user to launch nine or ten boilies at a time out to the baited area. By topping the rocket up with water once you have loaded it with boilies you will be able to reach the distant spots.

Spodding in Practice

Having the correct equipment not only means that you can deliver your bait to its intended target; it also means that the whole experience is less of a chore. This in turn means that you can concentrate on the more important things, such as accuracy. Having discussed the basic gear you will need for spodding, I want to look at how to get the best from it. You see, it is not just a long-range tactic; its applications can be many and varied.

To start with, I want to talk a little more about the spod itself. Modern-day spods have been designed to be as aerodynamic and stable as possible: the better the spod's stability in flight, the further it will go. Sounds very obvious, doesn't it, but I often see anglers cutting down their range by overfilling them. It is very easy to understand why this happens. Spodding is a physically demanding technique, especially at range, and we all want each spod-load to carry as much

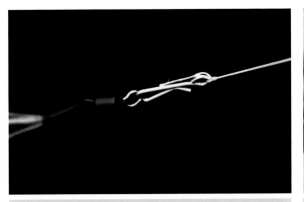

A quick-change clip helps to change the spods quickly.

Interchangeable nose cones mean that I can always see the spod.

bait as possible. There is nothing more frustrating than seeing a spod wobbling about all over the place and landing short of the mark. A wasted cast and a waste of bait! Worse still, dropping spod-loads of bait away from the intended target area may take the carps' attention away from the main baited area and ruin your chances of a take or two. Never fill the spod right to the top as this is a sure-fire way to make it unstable. Instead, leave about an inch and a half free at the top of the spod once you have filled it. This ensures that the majority of the weight is concentrated towards the front end, and helps to keep the flight straight and true. It also has the added bonus of reducing 'spod spill', a subject I will come back to in a little while.

Don't overfill the spod.

In the main, spods come in two different sizes, large and small. The first and most obvious choice arising from this is the amount of bait that you wish to introduce. There is also the fact that you may wish to make slightly less disturbance with the use of a smaller spod. I tend to use the larger ones, because I can deliver the same amount of bait with one large one as I can with two smaller loads. Disturbance isn't a problem for me and I

The two different spod sizes.

will explain why and how I overcome this. Very often, when you watch anglers spodding, the spod itself lands in the water with an almighty splash, which is not really the ideal way to introduce bait. I have a method of minimising this splash as much as possible, almost to the point at which I cannot actually hear the thing land in the water. Once I am happy that I have the right range via a couple of practice casts, I simply strip off a couple of extra yards of line and put it in the line clip. (These are positioned on the side of the spool on most modern reels.) The spod is then loaded and I aim to cast 5 to 10 yards beyond the marker float. With the spod in flight, I keep the rod up high and, as the line tightens to the clip, I lower the rod, carefully lowering the spod onto the surface of the water. This technique requires some practice, but once mastered it becomes very satisfying to put out a large amount of bait with hardly a ripple on the surface. This use of the line clip has another useful side-effect. If you want to re-bait your spots or simply top them up, then you only have to line your spot up with a distant marker and cast it out to the clip. Job done! If you ensure that you put a marker on the line of the rods you are fishing with then, at night, once more using a skyline marker, you can re-cast your hook bait accurately and bait up again with the spod. It takes all the guesswork out of it, and once more you are back in the ball game. Learning these tactics and techniques takes a little patience, but once you have mastered them life becomes so much easier.

I have already touched on the matter of not overloading the spod, but before we look at the loading process in more detail, I think it best to discuss what happens on the bank first. As much as I love watching the wildlife when I am on the bank, I don't think I am alone when I say that I hate having water birds in and around my lines when I am fishing. They really can spoil a good day. In order to avoid this, and also of course to ensure their safety, the best option is to give them no reason to come visiting your margin. To this end, I always load my spod well away from the water's edge. That way I can ensure that none of the bait falls in. Sure, the birds may come in for a look, but when they find nothing to eat, they will move on to annoy the angler next door! I also try not to allow the spod to swing out over the water, as small items may fall out there too. I'm not bothered about small crumbs of bait falling onto the bank. Robins I can handle; swans I cannot! With the birds at arm's length we can concentrate on the job in hand.

A lot of my fishing is done with boilies and pellets only. The one problem with spodding boilies is that they will jam in a large spod, and are very often not released. It is incredibly frustrating to retrieve a spod full of bait! I found that the use of a mixture of different sized baits helped (e.g. 10 mm and 14 mm boilies), but it was not infallible. The inclusion of a small amount of pellets, however, ensured that the boilies were separated enough to allow their release every time. The pellets have one other useful role to fulfil, and that is to plug the end of the spod to avoid spod spill. Not only is spod spill a great waste of bait, it encourages the birds to dive around your lines and also gives the carp another area to focus their attentions on.

What I do on arrival at the venue is to half-fill a large maggot container with pellets and cover them with water. I leave them for five minutes and drain off the excess. By the time I am sorted out

Robins I can handle; swans I cannot.

Fill the spod, leaving two inches at the top.

and ready to bait-up, the pellets have become soft enough to form a light paste. I then fill the spod to about two inches from the top and use half an inch of the paste to cap it. Not only does this eliminate spod spill, it also helps to concentrate the weight of the bait to the nose of the spod and helps it fly straight and true. The force of the impact with the water ensures the bait is pushed out, but I do leave the spod in position for a few seconds just to be satisfied that it has completely emptied. So, that is basically how I go about spodding boilies and pellets. However, there is plenty more to look at. Small light items such as seeds, maggots and casters cause their own problems, so let's tackle these.

Take a small amount of the damp pellets.

Now plug the spod.

It is now ready to go.

I keep saying it, but it is always important to ensure that the spod is filled to the correct level and the weight of the bait is concentrated towards the nose. Problems arise when we try to spod out lighter items. Let's use maggots as an example, then what I am about to suggest can be used with similar items. Just so that you are sure what I am talking about here, think about a spod full of boilies and how much lighter a similar volume of maggots would weigh. At shorter ranges, say 40 or 50 yards, I can simply insert the blanking cylinder into my spod and use a small amount of paste to stop them falling out. However, when I go for the longer ranges, the lightness of the maggots doesn't allow me to make the distance, and the plug makes the spod unstable. This is where a more dedicated spod mix comes into play. I have already outlined this mix in the previous chapter of the book, so I will not reiterate it here. What it does though, is add casting weight, which allows me to include a lot of maggots in with it. Also, by adding a small quantity of pellets to the mix, I can make it quite stodgy. This negates the need to use the pellet paste to plug the bait into the spod.

Before moving on, I can't leave the subject of spodding without talking about one particular tactic that I use it for. I call it 'dappling', which is basically the art of introducing bait to a margin spot via the spod. There is no need to cast when doing this; just swing the spod into position on a long line. Catapults are fine some of the time, but have you seen what happens to varying sized baits when they are fired out against a strong wind? They go all over the place. Baiting spoons (which are basically large, purpose-made ladles that screw into the end of a pole) are fine, but the length of

A dedicated spod mix adds weight and allows me to use maggots at range.

Dappling, silent but deadly.

the pole to which they are attached limits you somewhat. Since dappling doesn't involve casting, it means you have total control over the spod so that it doesn't crash down onto the surface. It also means that, if you are using multiple-sized bait items, they are dropped very accurately onto the spot. Silent but deadly!

Groundbait Sling

This is probably the most underused tactic of all. Why, I have no idea, because it has the potential to deliver bait by rod at incredible distances. It has the ability to out-cast a spod and is far less strenuous. I have detailed the groundbait mixes that I use in the previous chapter, but I will make the point again that the groundbait balls will need to be dried for a couple of hours just to harden them up a little. They will be travelling at tremendous speed and hardening them slightly means that they will survive without breaking up.

The equipment you need is exactly the same as for spodding. The only difference here is that you will be tying a groundbait sling, not a spod, on the end of your line. The actual sling resembles the pouch found on a groundbait catapult – indeed, the first one I ever used was taken from just such a catapult. They are now, of course, commercially available. All you do is place one of the groundbait balls into the sling, aim at the spot where you want it to land, and cast. The real beauty of this is that, unlike spodding, you don't have to reel in. The sling will literally flutter down onto the water just beyond your rod tip, and you then repeat the process. If you are lucky enough to have someone around who can place the bait in the sling, the process is made so much easier. It will take some practice, and making up the groundbait does take a little time, but it will be worth it in the end!

Remote-controlled Bait Boat

Love them or hate them, the remote-controlled bait boat is here to stay. As technology advances, so it finds its way into the world of fishing. Remote-controlled boats are one such advance. Today, we accept the hair rig as just a normal part of carp fishing. It would surprise a great many anglers of today, who were not around when the hair rig came out, just how much criticism it came in for. 'Like shooting ducks at a fairground', someone very famously described it. Many thought that the art of angling was lost because the angler no longer needed to set the hook himself. Striking a fish is, for the traditionalist, as integral a part of carp fishing as the skill of casting.

The groundbait sling in action.

Bait boats are here to stay.

I once did an article about the use of bait boats on a lake where they are commonplace. At the time, it was a subject that many angling writers shied away from. In an effort to understand this thorny issue a little better, I talked at length to the lake owner. He explained that, in years gone by, most of his time was taken up with removing items of tackle that had been cast into the trees on the many islands the lake contains. The dangers to the wildlife were obvious, and in an effort to control this he allowed bait boats to be used. He no longer has to worry about such things.

Most of the criticism about bait boats seems to revolve around the fact that these remarkable devices are open to abuse by the angler. It is for this reason that there are many waters that do not allow their use. If you decide that you want to use one, then please bear the following in mind. Never use them to deliver hook baits into snags or other places where they would put the carp at risk. The welfare of the fish must be uppermost in your mind. Always show courtesy for the other anglers on the lake. With a bait boat you will be able to take baits to distant points unreachable when casting. The danger here is that you will be

encroaching into other anglers' swims. Not only is this extremely bad angling, it also encourages an extremely bad environment in which to relax and fish.

Having said all that, there are plenty of plus points regarding their use. Bait and hook bait delivery can be achieved with unparalleled accuracy, and with the minimum of disturbance. If, for instance, you can see fish milling around in a certain area then the boat is far less likely to disturb them than the sound of a lead and bait hitting the water. Couple this with the fact that you won't need more than one attempt at positioning the bait, and you can begin to see why these things are so devastating. Without doubt, when a water is first opened up to their use, the results can be beyond belief.

Over the course of time however, the carp will eventually move the goalposts. All too soon they become familiar with the very tight baiting pattern and start to feed with greater caution. This is when the angler has to start thinking once again. Just because a bait boat can carry a considerable quantity of bait, that doesn't mean that you have to put a whole load out every time. Maybe it will be a case of running the boat

Just because bait boats can carry lots of bait doesn't mean that you have to fill them up all the time.

out a few times to deliver smaller amounts of bait over a wider area. Maybe dropping the bait while the boat is on the move will help to spread it out a little more. Predictability, whatever we are doing, it will ultimately lead to some carp getting away with a free meal!

Modern bait boats come with other interesting additions. Some now come with a fish-finder. Now I would take that title with a pinch of salt, because it has been my experience that they are nothing of the sort. Any bits of flotsam and jetsam can register as a fish and this can be very misleading. In fact, what they do best of all is act as a feature-finder. Gravel bars and plateaux show up well and leave you in no doubt where to put the hook bait. Some now even come with GPS system, and this takes any guesswork out of re-positioning the hook baits! Used sensibly, there are no problems with bait boats. Have the utmost respect for the carp you are targeting and the other anglers, then much of the negative stigma will be forgotten.

10 ESTABLISHING A BAIT

Before we look at how to get your chosen bait established in the venue you have selected, I think it best to discuss why it is important to do so. I have read over and over again that if you offer the fish the bare minimum of bait, this increases the chance of your hook bait being picked up. I am not going to argue that point here, but I find it much better to establish a bait in a venue, then gain the carps' confidence in eating it. A small amount of bait may work in the short term, but the longevity of a bait can be increased greatly the more the carp feed on it without being caught.

As I explained in Chapter 2, carp are simple creatures steeped in millions of years of evolution, which means they have developed incredibly strong instincts. These instincts drive the carp to reproduce when the urge and weather conditions dictate, to be safe and comfortable in their environment, and to feed. Additional to a natural desire to feed is the carp's familiarity with its environment, which helps it to relocate established food sources at any given time. Carp are also fully capable of taking advantage of opportunist feeding and it is safe to say that they are capable of selecting food items which will help them to meet any dietary requirements. Above all, the less energy they have to expend in order to satisfy their nutritional requirements, the more readily carp will feed. So it seems safe to say that carp are simple

You've got what I want, so feed me.

It's not all doom and gloom.

creatures: sex once a year, spend time in safe and comfortable places and take advantage of any available food sources. Simple isn't it?

Well, to be honest with you, it isn't! The fact that we actually go fishing for them puts a major spanner in the works. Angling pressure will change these habits because of their overriding instinct for survival. Lines in the water, leads and spods crashing around their heads and bankside disturbance will all have an effect on their behaviour. The biggest problem is that the carp are getting caught occasionally. Again, the instinct for self-preservation kicks in, and the fish will be on its guard because of previous bad experiences. More often than not, carp feeding cautiously will get away with it. In extreme cases they may well avoid the baited areas all together. Now before you

run away, sell your carp gear and take up golf, all is not the doom and gloom that this may sound. Help is at hand.

Just because carp are wild creatures, steeped in thousands of years of self-preservation, this does not mean that, from time to time, we cannot condition them into doing exactly what we want them to do. And that is to eat our bait, and continue eating it. I have seen it mentioned that carp will only eat until they are nutritionally satisfied; in other words enough to fulfil their immediate nutritional requirements. In my experience and that of many of my friends, nothing could be further from the truth. Carp are incredibly greedy creatures and will eat until they are nearly at bursting point. What they are doing is taking advantage of an easy food source, and getting as much of it as they can while the going is good. They will eat more than most of us can imagine. Let me paint a little picture here.

Carp will eat until they are nearly bursting.

We have arrived at the lake and it contains about one hundred carp. It is highly unlikely that we will get all the fish feeding at any one time, so for argument's sake let's say we have twenty-five carp feeding in our swim. The bed of bait we have put out consists of 10 kilos of 18 mm boilies – at a rough guess, this would equate to about one thousand baits. Although it is unlikely, we'll say that all the fish are feeding with the same intensity, which works out at forty boilies each. You are going to have to take my word for it, but I have seen a single carp eat ten times that amount of bait in just a few short minutes!

Okay then. So far we have established that carp are simple creatures and that they can eat an incredible amount of bait. You would be forgiven, therefore, for thinking that it was just a case of turning up at the lake, piling in the bait then sitting back and waiting for your indicators to start dancing. Unfortunately, fishing is very rarely that easy. First of all we have to consider a few things. I have mentioned some of these before, but they are relevant here, too.

1. How much time and money can you invest in a baiting campaign?

2. What bait should you be using?

3. Is it possible to get a friend, or friends, involved to spread the work and cost?

4. How much angling pressure is there on the venue?

Getting a friend involved helps to spread the cost.

These are all important points that you will need to give some thought to. For me though, the most important question is: 'Where shall I put that bait to get the maximum benefit from its application?' Indiscriminate baiting will invariably cost you a great deal of money and frustration. Think long and hard before you begin applying your bait!

Once you have considered all these points, it is time to look at what bait you are going to use. We are talking here about establishing a bait, and its long-term use. I described the characteristics of ready-made or shelf-life boilies in Chapter 8. Relying as they do on their attractors and not their food content, I have never felt they are any good for long-term use. For the purposes of this chapter I will refer only to freezer or food source baits. If you intend to establish a bait, then you will have to look a little further than one that simply smells nice!

I have seen numerous anglers in tackle shops picking up a bag of bait and, because it smells nice to them, they automatically think it will be okay for the carp. Wrong! Long-term bait application is based on more than a nice smell. The food content of the bait is everything. Carp are extremely selective eaters, and they have not become so by eating things that are not doing them any good. Any bait we use has to compete with

> Freezer baits are the best for long-term application.

the natural food resources that the water contains. The more nutritional a bait is, the more likely the carp are to feed on it. And don't forget what I said earlier; a carp will exploit any available food source, particularly if it does not have to expend too much energy on foraging for it. Provided it is acceptable as a food source, the more a carp sees of it, the more regularly it will be eaten.

So, precisely which bait do you use? A huge part of carp fishing is having confidence in the bait you are using. If you are already using a bait that gives you confidence, then why change? If in doubt, however, take a look at the bait history of the water, at what baits have been successful in the past. The local grapevine should provide you with all the answers you need.

You will look just fine holding up the carp of your dreams…

One other point that I realise is relevant here concerns the cost. I am only too aware of the favoured position I am in with regard to bait, but it was not always so. For most of my carp fishing life, I have had to invest all my hard-earned cash into bait. It became obvious to me early on that, if I took shortcuts on bait, then my catch rates would suffer as a consequence. I am constantly amazed that anglers will spend thousands of pounds on all the latest tackle, and as little as possible on bait. Sure, all the latest trendy gear looks good on the bank, but it will all be irrelevant if you are not using a bait that the carp want to eat. On the other hand, trendy gear or not, you will look just fine when you are holding up the carp of your dreams for the camera! Keep in mind that, if money is a real issue for you, a good bait is far more likely to catch you carp than the latest camo bivvy table!

Right, then. You have made the decision and the bait has been made, ordered and delivered. The freezer is now bursting at the seams. It is what you do next that will make the difference between success and failure. One of the biggest mental blocks anglers have is that they feel they will be baiting-up only for others to take advantage of their hard work. Unfortunately, this is going to be the case at times. It's unavoidable. But a baiting campaign should not be undertaken with the short term in mind.

Now is the time that the hard work begins. You need to be putting your bait into as many areas as possible, but you must be sure that these are areas the carp visit and will feed on. Only by spending time at the venue will you be able to identify these areas of interest. Look again at the water's history, and it will probably tell you which areas have been good in the past. The good old MK 1 eyeball is by far your most important weapon at this stage. The more time you spend at the venue and the more you look, the more the carp will give the game away. Fizzing, leaping and bubbling carp will, at the very least, give you some spots to investigate – and investigate them you must. It will do wonders for your confidence if you can find out why the carp are interested in a particular area and the knowledge will, in future, help you to set your traps accordingly.

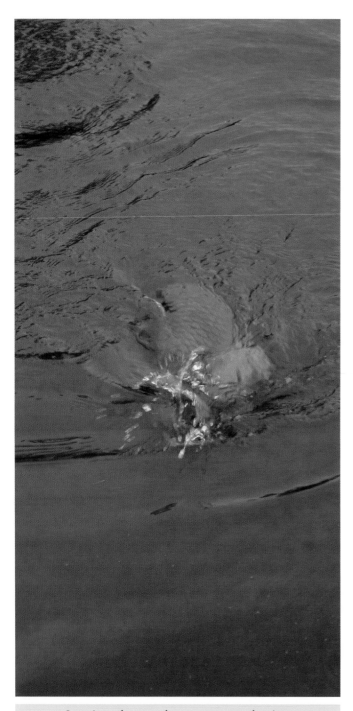

Investigate the area where you see carp showing.

When you are visiting the venue looking for feeding spots, never do so without your marker float rod. When you identify feeding areas it is essential to mark your line on the marker rod and the spod rod. Use electrical tape or magic marker braid in different colours, for different spots. Then all you do when you want to bait-up is cast the distance of the marker on the line, put the line in the reel clip and away you go. Try to find, and feed fish in the margins. That's the best way to gauge their reactions to your bait. To see fish devouring your bait is a massive confidence booster.

Record all the information you glean during these visits in a notebook; don't rely on memory, it often lets you down. This information will be useful when you come to actually fishing.

One thing to keep in mind is that, if you become aware that someone else is baiting-up the lake, then you may need to adjust your own tactics a little. If there is too much bait going into the water it could ruin things, especially in winter. However, when I think back, it hasn't been often that I have encountered this problem. I can't help feeling that many are missing out on so much.

Never visit the venue without your marker float rod.

The feeling of satisfaction when a plan comes together is indescribable.

A baiting campaign gives those who can be bothered a massive advantage. Hard work is all too often a phrase that some carp anglers don't want to hear. But believe me, the feeling of satisfaction when a plan comes together is indescribable.

How much bait should you be using? Through many years of frustration and sacrifice, I have got myself into the very fortunate position that I can use as much bait as I want to. I make no apology for that, because arriving here has been extremely hard work. However, for many, many years I was in exactly the same position as most readers of this book, so I can speak with good authority on the subject. Those of you working on a budget will be encouraged to know that, more important than the amount of bait, is the regularity with which you put it in. The bottom line though, is that the more they see of it without getting caught, the more they will come back for it.

To talk more specifically about quantities, let's go back to the lake mentioned earlier, the one with a hundred carp in it. As a rough guide I would be looking to get between 5 and 10 kilos of bait into the water once a week. That will, at the very least, give most of the fish a chance to get a taste for it. It is difficult to say when to put the bait in because everyone will have different constraints to work around. For instance, what time of day can you get to the lake, and how often? If you can get there every day then it is best to trickle small amounts of bait into your chosen spots. If you can only get there once or twice a week then you are going to have to introduce a fair bit more bait each time. And remember to take into account the other species of fish in the lake, and to some extent the bird life. They will come to the party, invited or not! Personally, I like to bait-up at night. Not only does this put other anglers off the scent, it also confuses the dreaded tufted ducks and coots, so the carp will at least get some time to enjoy the feast. Once you are fishing it is just as important to keep the bait going in. Remember, if they keep seeing it, they will invariably get caught more than once on that particular bait.

Other species will come to the party…invited or not.

Carp are the best judges of whether a bait is good or not.

So, what have we discovered then? That carp are simple, wild creatures and we can encourage them to do what we want them to — within reason! They will eat far more bait than most of us can imagine, and the more they eat our bait, the more likely we are to catch them.

What I have tried to do here is to set the scene and give you some ideas to think about before you invest a large amount of time, money and effort. You may have decided already that this is not for you. Be mindful though, that you will get very little out of your fishing if you are not prepared to walk that extra mile from time to time. Simply doing what everyone else is doing means that you will only catch what they are catching. Top quality bait is everything. Carp are the best judges of whether a bait is good or not. Get them eating the right bait, then keep them feeding on it, and they will continue to get caught.

11

PVA PRODUCTS

There can be little doubt that PVA has been one of the most significant carp fishing developments of recent years. PVA stands for polyvinyl acetate. Basically, it is a material that will dissolve when immersed in water. Once dissolved, it leaves no discernible residue and is not harmful to the environment or the fish. Its use has opened up a

A stunning mirror, courtesy of PVA.

whole myriad of different presentations and these help to keep the carp guessing. By varying our presentation we ensure that the carp are not becoming accustomed to one particular set of circumstances, and therefore they will be easier to catch. Over the years, and as clever carp fishing minds have set to work, the choices have become almost endless and are limited only by our own imagination.

So what are we trying to achieve with the use of PVA? First and foremost, it allows us to have free offerings in the immediate vicinity of our hook bait. These can be fished alone or in amongst a larger baited area. Either way, this presentation seems to focus the fish on the area where the hook bait is and helps to make the carp more catchable. The use of this product also helps to eliminate tangles, as the increased weight at the hook end stops the hooklink tangling around the main line. It also protects the hook point when we are fishing over gravel. Nice!

PVA comes in a multitude of different configurations.

PVA comes in a multitude of different configurations: string, tape, solid bags of various sizes, stocking or mesh material plus dissolving foam. But a word of warning before I carry on. Since PVA is designed to melt when it comes into contact with water, it stands to reason that it needs to be looked after and kept dry in amongst your other tackle. When you are attempting to attach bait to it, or place bait in it, the bait will need to be dry or, at the very least, covered in a substance that will not melt the PVA. (I will cover this point in more depth when I look at the baits used with PVA products.) It stands to reason that your hands also need to be dry. One last point is that you will have to ensure that whatever you attach your PVA product to will also need to be totally dry. There is nothing more frustrating than going to a lot of effort, only for the product to disintegrate before you cast out!

String and Tape

The first type of presentation that involved the use of a PVA product was called the stringer. This was developed around the early nineteen-eighties and was to have a massive influence, as it still does to this day. As the name suggests, the stringer is constructed from a short length of PVA string or tape. All that is needed to make this is a long stringer needle and a length of PVA string or tape that will allow you to thread the required number of baits onto it. I must admit that I find tape is better than string. Its width allows the baits to remain separated without the use of any knots. This is important, as the exposed PVA will melt quickly and allow the free offerings to separate on the lake bed.

Now, although the basic stringer is a very effective tactic, there are countless variations and tricks that we can use to give us even more of an edge. On today's busy waters, where the carp will have seen a vast selection of the more normal presentations, we need to be a little more thoughtful. Remember that carp, although they don't have a thought process as we know it, can learn easily by association. Once they have been caught a couple of times on a certain set-up, they very quickly associate that with danger, which lessens the chances of them picking up a similarly presented hook bait. However, the list of options is almost endless and, by experimenting with the different options, not only are you keeping your fishing interesting, you are making it more difficult for the carp to get away with a free meal!

What follows are a few ideas that I have used over the years to great effect.

To make the standard stringer, first thread four or five baits onto the stringer needle.

Double over the end of the tape and insert the crook of the stringer needle into that loop.

Now pull the baits individually onto the tape.

The last bait should now have the loop you formed first protruding from the top. Leave a gap of at least half an inch between each bait to allow the water to get at the tape.

Now insert the baited hook through the loop a couple of times. This will then survive a fairly strong cast.

The finished stringer will end up looking like the photo and will ensure that the free offerings will end up close to the hook.

As mentioned earlier, the basic stringer is still effective, but to make it just a little different we can turn that straight line of baits into a circle. Set up the baits on the stringer needle as before and thread the baits onto the tape, remembering to leave the gaps. Then, instead of forming a loop at one end you can now leave that as a single thread. Once the baits are on the tape you can tie the two ends with a simple overhand knot. This can now be attached to the baited hook and cast out.

Also, why limit yourself to just one stringer? By following the system first described, you can place as many stringers on the line as you want.

One very successful tactic that I have used and is aptly named, is the 'piles' presentation. Simply thread three baits onto you needle and thread them onto the tape. With the hook bait attached to the rig, tie the three baits around the hooklink with an overhand knot. All you have to do now is slide it down over the eye of the hook, and push the hook point through one of the exposed sections of the PVA. Not only does this ensure that the free offerings are as close to the hook bait as possible, it also helps to protect the hook point when fishing over gravel. One other bonus is that, if you are fishing into light weed, it ensures that your hook will not be masked by it.

Double hook baits are very popular and we can use PVA to make our free offerings similar to the hook bait. Once the baits have been threaded onto the tape, force the baits together to form pairs. Because the PVA inside them is not exposed to the water, the baits will be left in pairs on the lake bed. The carp will soon get used to finding double freebies and suspicion will be lowered.

Alternatively, in an effort to make stringer arrangements even more effective, why not use baits that have been broken in half? These can be threaded onto the tape in exactly the same way as whole baits. Not only is this slightly different from the norm, it also allows more of the flavours and attractors to leak out of the bait.

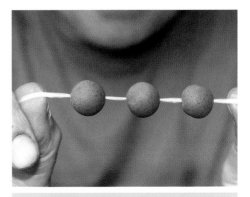
Thread three baits onto a length of PVA tape.

Tie the three baits around the hooklink.

Slide the baits down and push the point of the hook through one of the exposed sections.

PVA Bags

The next variation of PVA is the solid bag. This is perfect for a whole host of angling situations. PVA 'bagging' is ideal for short to mid-range fishing. Unfortunately, ranges over 80 yards are very hard to achieve because of the weight and bulk of a fully loaded bag. The use of PVA at longer ranges is a rather specialised subject and we will look at these techniques a little later in this chapter.

The PVA bag is a solid, non-porous film which, unlike mesh, allows the addition of oil-based liquid attractors. In addition to the normal bags, we can now get them carrying the flavours of the baits that we are using. These bags are not just simply flavoured, but harness the actual food liquids within the PVA film. As the bag dissolves, these unique scent trails disperse into the water, leaving a highly attractive cloud around the rig. These natural attractors provide a powerful signal for the carp to home in on.

PVA bags normally come in two different thicknesses to suit conditions. The thinner bags are ideal for all round use and winter-time, the thinner film helping the bag to dissolve quickly in cold water temperatures. The thicker material provides a slower melt rate and is designed for deeper water in summer temperatures. This heavier film ensures that the bag reaches the bottom intact without melting on the descent. (Early melting is a common problem with lighter, thinner bags, that can result in a wide spread of bait – not what the tactic is intended to achieve.) As a general guide, use the thinner film bags for winter fishing and for summer work in depths of no more than ten feet. The thicker-film bags should be used in summer for depths in excess of this, and for distance work where the extra thickness provides added strength. In addition to the thickness of the film, PVA bags come in various sizes. Obviously, the larger the bag, the more bait it will hold. However the larger the bag the less distance you will achieve on the cast: a large PVA bag will not be so aerodynamic.

A solid PVA bag in action.

Let's take a look at how I make up the basic PVA bag. I have also included a couple of items that are intended to make the construction much easier.

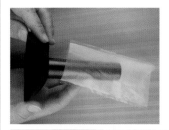

Using an Ezee Loader, first insert the funnel provided into the bag. (Ensure that all components are dry at this stage or they will cause problems later.)

Now place the lead weight into the little cup at the mouth of the funnel.

The baited hair and hooklink are now placed into the funnel so that the hook bait comes to rest at the bottom of the PVA bag. The hooklink should run through the slot in the cup that houses the lead.

The next job is to top up the bag with the bait that you intend to use. Fill the bag until it is three-quarters full.

At this stage I normally add a nugget of dissolving foam. This isn't essential, but once the bag melts it acts as a good sight marker if I wish to introduce any other free offerings. Carefully lower the lead down the funnel until it comes to rest on top of the bait.

You can add a little more bait at this stage, but not too much as you need the excess PVA to secure the bag.

Carefully remove the filled PVA bag and ease the main line out through the slot on the side of the Ezee Loader.

With a cotton bud, dampen the insides of the top of the bag. Be careful not to use too much liquid as this may melt the bag and you will have to start all over again!

Twist the top of the bag around the line, tubing or leadcore leader that you are using.

For added security, tie off the neck of the bag to the tubing or leader with PVA tape.

One final tip. If you want to make the bag a little more aerodynamic, simply lick the bottom corners of the bag and fold them into the bottom centre of the bag.

Standard PVA bags, as I have said, are fine for distances up to about 80 yards. However, when looking at ranges beyond that you will have to use smaller and more streamlined set-ups. Thankfully there are bags to accommodate this and that makes life so much easier. To achieve maximum distances the bags need to be as compact as possible, and the lead needs to be positioned at the bottom of the bag, not at the top.

If you intend to fish PVA bags at range then you also need to use the right rig. I outlined the helicopter rig in Chapter 7, so you will be aware of how it is constructed. You will also need to make the hooklink very short. Personally, I would not use one that was more than five or six inches in length. This may seem a little on the short side, but remember that when the carp is feeding on the contents of the bag it will not be moving around. The short hooklink ensures that the lead is brought into play as quickly as possible and aids in the hooking of the fish. Here's how I create my long-distance bag set-up.

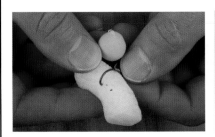

Start off by attaching a piece of dissolving foam to the point of the hook.

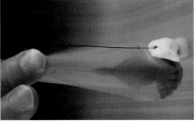

Place the lead in the tapered end of the bag. Ensure that the hooklink and hook bait are outside the bag.

Three-quarters fill the bag with your bait. You can use the Ezee Loader to do this if you wish.

Now put the hooklink into the bag. The hook bait should be at the top of the bag.

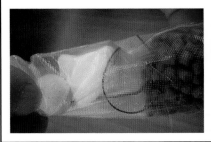

Squeeze the bag to remove as much air as possible. At the same time, start twisting the bag at the top. This helps to compact the contents further.

Secure with a knot of PVA tape.

Mesh Bags

These are my favourite form of PVA, mainly because they are so easy to use, but also because mesh allows the bags to be much more compact. Mesh comes on a tube in two different sizes and with refill packs available. One size is wide whilst the other is narrow and these sizes facilitate a range of options. One of the great advantages of this stuff is that you can make up a number of bags even before your session starts. This will leave more time for other important matters once you are on the bank.

Wide Mesh Bags

As I said, mesh is so easy to use and not only offers quick and easy bag construction, but also allows for a varied baiting strategy. So, where do we start?

  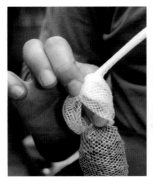 

First of all, ensure that the end of the mesh is knotted.

Now run the bait you intend to use down the tube.

Once all the bait is in the mesh you can start to compress it into a round ball.

Trapping the mesh in your fingers, start to twist it. This will further compress the bait.

Still gripping the bag with your fingers, form an overhand knot. Be careful to keep the tension on at this stage so that the contents don't become loose.

Once the knot has been tied, make another knot just above that one and you are ready to do the next one.

These bags can then be put on the baited hook and you are ready to cast out. Simple!

Because these bags are so compact, they can also be catapulted at fairly long range. With the hook bait surrounded by a small ball of bait, it is a good idea to catapult several of these bags around it. Hopefully the carp will gain the necessary confidence feeding on these bags to make a mistake with the one with the hook in it. If you find that you are not quite making the required distance, it is possible to put a stone in the bag to gain those extra yards. Please ensure that it is dry before you use it though!

Narrow Mesh Bags

By their nature, narrow mesh bags hold a lot less bait than their wider brethren. But, when the need arises, they can be used to make smaller, more subtle PVA traps. While they can be made up and used in the same way as the wider bags, there is more to them than that. They can be used to produce alternative forms of stringer, and the highly popular 'stick'.

Alternative Stringer
As with the PVA tape stringer, this method is used to put free offerings in the immediate vicinity of the hook bait.

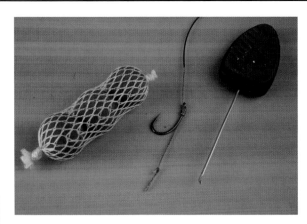

Put three or four boilies down the tube and into the mesh.

Twist the top to ensure the bait is held tightly.

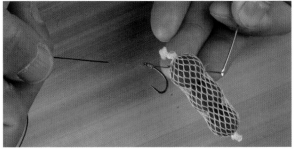

Now tie off the top, ensuring that you keep the pressure on the bait.

By using a baiting needle, one of the end boilies becomes the actual hook bait. (Of course, you can simply attach the narrow-meshed boilies to your hook if you so wish.)

Although they are not that aerodynamic, they can be used in this way to bait your area.

PVA Sticks

The PVA stick has become one of the most popular PVA methods since it first came to prominence a few years ago. Like all the other PVA techniques, the stick is very effective, as it can deliver a tight package of loose feed on or around the hook bait. It also helps to disguise a portion of the terminal tackle.

The whole method revolves around a simple 'funnel and plunger' system, which will create a tube of compacted bait. So compact in fact, that with the right ingredients, the bait literally explodes once the PVA starts to melt.

To construct the PVA sticks you will need a loaded funnel and plunger and a suitable bag/stick mix.

First tie a knot in the end of the mesh.

The funnel then needs to be filled with the required amount of bait.

How much you put in will dictate the size of the stick. As with any other form of PVA bag work, if distance is required then the bags will need to be smaller.

Place the knotted end of the funnel onto a hard, flat surface and compress the bait using the plunger. This process creates a compact package, which casts well, sinks quickly and breaks apart nicely on the lake bed.

Grip the mesh immediately above the contents as tightly as possible. Twisting it a couple of times will compress the bait further.

Keeping the tension on the mesh, now tie an overhand knot.

Tie another overhand knot just above the first and cut the mesh in between the two knots. You are then ready to tie another stick.

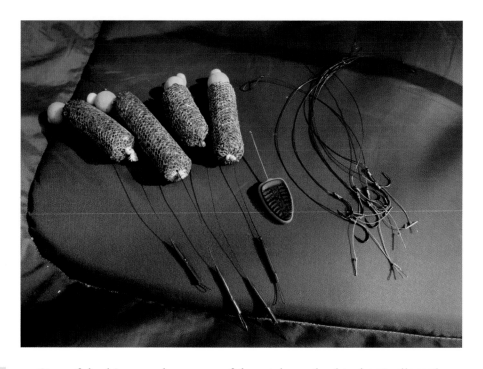

Ready-tied sticks.

One of the biggest advantages of the stick method is that it allows bags or mesh sticks to be made up in advance, and for hooklinks to be re-tied for the ultimate convenience. On more prolific venues, where regular action can be expected, this is great help. Simply unclip the used rig and, if the hook is still sharp, thread up another stick, attach it and cast back out. It is also possible to make up several spare hooklinks with the sticks already mounted and hook baits attached. These can be stored in the bait bucket. As and when fish are caught, you simply unclip the old rig and attach a new one, then you are very quickly back in the ball game!

In order for the stick to be threaded onto the hooklink with the minimum of fuss, there are several things we need to do and use that were not covered in the chapter on rigs.

For the following example I have used a lead clip and pendulum lead. This is my personal choice – other lead set-ups can be used. There are no limits to the hooking arrangement that you can use, but at the other end of the hooklink you will have to form a small loop by way of a figure of eight knot. Also, it is always best to use Kwik Change Swivels and Anti-Tangle Sleeves when using PVA sticks.

First of all thread the Anti-Tangle Sleeve onto the stringer needle. Thread the stringer needle through the full length of the stick.

Place the loop formed on the end of the hooklink onto the end of the stringer needle and carefully draw it back through the stick.

Now secure the hook in the end of the stick. Be careful not to put it into the knot as this may not dissolve fully and could thus mask the hook point.
Thread the sleeve off the needle and onto the hooklink.

Dissolving Foam

As far as I am aware this material was first used in the packaging industry. You know, the stuff that somewhat annoyingly gets spread all over your house when you unpack a parcel! A word of warning though – not all the packaging is water-soluble so, if you want to use that form of it, check that it melts first! Eventually some bright spark realised how useful this could be in a fishing situation. I, for one, am very grateful.

By attaching a piece to your hook before casting out, two things will happen. First of all, because of the buoyant nature of this material, it will hold the hook and hook bait off the bottom to the extent of the hooklink. This allows the rig to settle gently on the bottom, thus avoiding any bottom debris. (Much will depend on the size and

Dissolving foam.

buoyancy of the hook bait here, but even large baits will have their descent to the bottom slowed to some degree.) Second, when the little nugget floats to the surface, it can be used as a target for the introduction of free offerings. At the very least, if you intend to spod to a marker float you will know where your rig is in relation to that float.

The foam nuggets also help to streamline your rigs, especially in the case of longer hairs. These can be a real pain because they tend to induce tangles. By trapping the hair to the shank and bend of the hook this can be avoided. Moulding a nugget of foam around the hook point will also help to protect it from damage by gravel and other abrasive material. The best way I have found of putting the foam on the hook is to take a piece and compress it slightly. Now slightly moisten one side. Impale the middle on the hook point and fold the ends around the shank and

Slightly compress and moisten a nugget of foam.

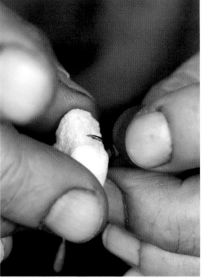

Impale it on the hook, through the middle.

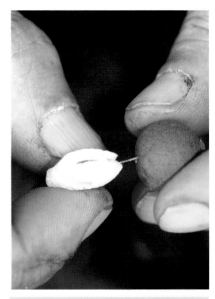

Fold the ends around the shank and hair.

the hair. Leave it for a few seconds for the two sides to bond, then cast out.

So there you have it. A fairly basic but concise guide to the use of PVA products. There is little doubt in my mind that this material will continue to be very effective. Its only limitation is the limit of our own imagination. Experimenting for ourselves is one of the most satisfying parts of carp fishing and with some thought I am sure we can take this method even further.

Experimenting for ourselves is one of the most satisfying parts of carp fishing.

12 STALKING

Stalking is probably one of the most underused methods of carp fishing. There may be many reasons for this, but perhaps the most obvious is that carp anglers are encouraged to spend hundreds, if not thousands, of pounds on their gear. Once in possession of the latest bivvy, matching rods and bite alarms, it is understandable that the angler wants to use them as often as possible. However, I am always amazed by anglers who say they have no time for stalking – or surface fishing for that matter – commenting that it takes too long to get a bite. Yet those same anglers will spend twenty-four hours, and longer, behind a matching set of rods waiting for a take. It is each to his own of course, but try not to limit yourself to one tactic alone. You will be missing out on so much.

Stalking is a tactic that is probably best suited to the warmer months, although I have caught a lot of carp stalking in the winter. It is, however, very dependent on climatic conditions in the colder months. So, for the most part, I want to look at stalking during the warmer times of the year, and April is a good month to start. As winter turns to spring, Mother Nature is rejuvenating herself, the weather is warming and the wildlife will be at their most vibrant. At the very least, the annoying, bait-stealing coots and other waterfowl will be more interested in getting their collective legs over than bothering to pick up my bait! More important, though, is the fact that the carp will be very much awake. The longer days mean that the sun has an increased warming effect on the water, encouraging the fish to forage for food on a wider scale. Their natural larders will begin to fill up as the insects and invertebrates once again start to reproduce. Although sexual activity is some way off, the carp will be feeding up in readiness for the spawning ritual, a time when they will need all of their strength. It is now that the shallower areas of the water will warm up the quickest. Not only will the carp enjoy basking in the warmer water, they will also take full advantage of the natural food to be found there. The biggest and shallowest feature on most of the venues that we fish is the margin. And for the patient, stealthy carp angler this is a time of plenty.

Without doubt, stalking is my favourite style of carp fishing for a number of reasons. When we are fishing open water at 50, 60, or 70 yards we do the best we can to get a take. The marker float has found us a nice feature, we have baited with pinpoint accuracy and the hook baits have been positioned accordingly. Once this kind of trap has been set, we are waiting for the carp to complete the equation, and there is little else we can do. Stalking the margins opens up a whole different ball game. The ability to actually see the carp feeding and going about their everyday lives gives you so much more information on which to base your traps. Favourite areas can be isolated and you can observe closely the way in which the carp are feeding. How many carp are feeding and what is their reaction to any bait you have introduced? Even the direction from which they approach the area will give you valuable

As the weather warms, the carp will move into shallow water.

For the patient and stealthy angler, this is a time of plenty.

information when considering where to put the hook bait. Stalking is also one of the best ways of isolating and catching the bigger fish. All that aside, this method is so visually exciting that it is guaranteed to get the old pulse rate soaring. It can also be very frustrating at times, but that only adds to the excitement for me. Any frustration will be forgotten when it all comes together, and you are playing a stalked fish with your heart in your mouth. It really doesn't get any better. Finally, one of the biggest benefits of spending time eyeball to eyeball with your quarry is that you will learn far more about them than if you constantly remain static behind a battery of rods. Knowledge is power!

I have been fortunate in that many of the lakes that I have frequented have lent themselves to this style of fishing. The clear, shallow and weedy margins of Wraysbury, Horton Church Lake, Yateley Car Park Lake and Conningbrook have taught me so much. These lakes are amongst the hardest in the angling world. The low stocks of big carp they contain have seen it all over the years, and are very used to being fished for in the edge. As you can imagine, they are always on their guard. After all, big carp were once little carp and if they swam into the margins as fingerlings they were very likely to be targeted by predators, herons

It is good to watch the carp going about their business.

being just one example. Carp feel exposed when they come into shallow water, and their instincts for survival remain throughout their lives, even though a hungry heron is going to have its work cut out to swallow a 30 lb carp! So, the first thing we need to ensure is that the carp do not detect us. Alerting them to our presence is one sure-fire way of sending them scurrying out of the area, leaving us nothing to fish for.

Pressured, low-stocked lakes have taught me so much.

The Approach

Invariably, on arrival at any water I will go for a walk around it first. If it is one of those waters that lends itself to stalking, I will have a made-up rod, landing net, unhooking mat and a few bits and pieces with me, just in case I happen across some carp on my travels. There is nothing more frustrating than finding one of these opportunities, only to have to return to your car for the equipment. The chance will be missed. If I don't see anything to fish for, then at least I can use the equipment to secure a swim if one takes my fancy. However, the gear is with me primarily to take advantage of any situations I find in the margins – situations that can be ruined by a heavy-footed approach.

In many respects, the most important piece of equipment at this stage

Polarised sunglasses and a peaked cap – vital!

is a decent set of Polaroid sunglasses. It is hard to emphasise enough just how crucial these are. Taking the glare from the surface of the water improves your vision immeasurably. Couple these with a peaked cap, and you have removed the need to keep raising your hand to shield your eyes – a movement that could potentially spook any carp present. Further to this, think about your clothing. It is not really necessary to make yourself look like a tree to go stalking; drab clothing in browns and greens is good enough. It is your silhouette, shape, and movement that are more likely to give you away – and, of course, noise. Stalking is a game that requires extreme patience. Blundering up to the water's edge with heavy footfalls and snapping twigs is certain to frighten off the fish.

Be sure to check even the unlikely spots.

If the water isn't too big, I will investigate all the likely (and some unlikely) looking areas. A few of the features will be blindingly obvious. Overhanging trees, snags and reed beds are all areas that carp love to frequent. They provide cover plus a degree of security. Often though, I have found fish in a totally open area. It may just be that they feel comfortable there, but I suspect that it will have a lot to do with food, be it natural or even discarded bait left by a departing angler. I have lost count of the times I have seen carp anglers tip their left-over bait into the margins, and this is just one more reason why carp find the edges so alluring.

So, be sure to look everywhere, ensuring that all movement is slow and deliberate. Try to concentrate on where you place your feet and, once in position, remain as still as you can. Any sudden movements, and you may have to go looking for them all over again!

Climbing trees is one of the best ways to spot fish.

Climbing trees is one of the best ways of spotting fish. The elevation will give you an unrivalled view of the lake and its inhabitants. The topography of the lake bed will also be more visible. Weed beds and clear spots will be easier to see and, most important of all, the way the carp are using these features. (Please be careful when climbing trees; the danger of serious injury is very real. Also, ensure that the fishery rules allow you to do this. You don't want to get thrown out of the gate just as it's getting interesting!) Finding and watching the carp is only the start of it though. Now is the time to bite the bullet and take your time. Patience, once again, is a real virtue.

In a perfect world, we would find the fish and isolate the feeding spot. The carp would then swim off and give us time to introduce the hook bait and any free offerings we felt necessary. The problem with stalking, however, is that the situation is rarely perfect. And that, in essence, is what

A well-used spot in the margin.

makes it so incredibly exciting. The scenarios are potentially endless, so it is difficult for me to give you specific examples. In general, however, the things that you should be looking for are any spots that the carp are visiting frequently, the routes they are taking in and out of the area and any other evident patterns to their behaviour. Above all, you are trying to find the opportunity to introduce free offerings and to place your hook bait.

What follows is the sixty-four thousand dollar question. Should you actually put in any free offerings at all, and should you put your hook bait in at the same time? It could turn out that you get no feeding response. In this instance, it may be a case of baiting-up and visiting the area from time to time to see if the bait is still there. For the sake of argument, let's assume that the carp are giving you at least a little hope. In the short term, in this situation, I have never found that a lot of bait gives much benefit. If the carp turn their backs for a while and you pile a load of bait on the chosen spot, it very often frightens them, and they will bolt to the far side of the lake. Better, I feel, just to put a small amount in, say twenty or thirty pellets or five or six boilies broken into quarters: just enough to grab their attention, but not enough to scare them off. Remember, in all likelihood, we are looking for one take at best from these spots. The ensuing disturbance caused by a hooked fish will probably ensure that the rest will not return for some while. Unfortunately, even the introduction of the tiniest amount of bait will be, at times, enough for them not to return, and in such circumstances a single hook bait will be the best option. Experience, I'm afraid, is the only thing that can help you decide. All I can say by way of guidance is that if the fish are actively seeking food you may well get away with adding some bait. If they are not, then the introduction of a single hook bait may well elicit a pick up born of curiosity. It's really down to trial and error. But, as I said earlier, stalking is the best way to find out how the carp in your chosen venue respond to different situations. This knowledge will be invaluable in the future. You should always let the carp tell you where, and how, you should be fishing, and stalking is no different. In saying that, this is what I find so attractive about stalking the margins: I am constantly learning and seeking ways to overcome challenges.

Positioning

The next important thing is to decide on the position you are going to fish from. Make sure that you can at least get a little comfortable, so you are not continually twitching around. A stalking chair is ideal, but not always possible to position. In fact, I find them a hindrance at times. Once more or less comfortable, the next thing to do is to set up the landing net and make sure that it is easily to hand. This seems another blindingly obvious thing to say, but you don't want to be fumbling for it – let alone trying to set it up – with an angry carp tearing around on the end of your line. Finally, give a little thought as to where you are going to set the rod down. You do not want to position the hook bait and then start dithering around for somewhere to put your rod. The key word here is organisation. Now, I understand as well as anyone that when you have carp feeding on your spot it is very hard to think straight. All rational thought deserts you. But organised you must be, if you are to get the best from this situation.

A True-life Example

As I said, there are many variables to stalking, so I would like to tell you about one of the many captures I have made whilst using this method. This story encompasses just about all that I have been explaining so far.

I had arrived at a small syndicate lake and, as per normal, set out on a circuit of the lake. With no other anglers present, I could take my time. Try as I might, I could not find any fish in the edge – or anywhere else for that matter. Eventually, with nothing else to go on, I set up, and fished the middle of the seven-acre estate lake.

I was awake just before first light and, having had no action in the night I started out once again to look for signs. I didn't need to travel too far. Fifty yards down to my right, I spotted several fish mooching around a small patch of weed, right in the margin and no more than five feet from the bank. With no natural cover or trees to climb, I had to settle for crawling on my belly to get into a position to see what was going on. I made myself comfortable and settled down to watch. The lack of elevation meant that it was some time before I could actually make out what was going on. They seemed to be in a feeding mood, but were not exactly going mad. After about an hour, I discovered that the carp were dipping down on one particular spot directly behind the weed bed. Thankfully, they were constantly on the move, and at the furthest point of their travels they were no more than ten yards from the spot. The weed bed, I hoped, would conceal any of my movements from the fish. Once they had moved away from there I would be able to get the hook bait in position. At no point did I introduce any free offerings.

The weed bed also gave me a good indication of how I should conceal my line. I certainly did not want my line to be draping over the top of it. What I intended to do was lower the rig over the weed, run the length of leadcore along the bottom of it and position the rod a few yards to the right. I crept slowly back to my stalking rod and gear. On the hair, I had baited with two 10 mm boilies, onto which I connected a walnut-sized PVA bag of pellets. Just a mouthful and, hopefully, enough to get a bite.

Ever so slowly, I crept back into position and waited for the carp to move to the far side of the weed. I lowered the end tackle into position with barely a ripple on the surface. Keeping the bale arm of the reel open, I moved slowly to the right, laying the line along the bottom of the weed. I slackened off the line and engaged the free-spool facility. Job done.

It appeared that the carp were none the wiser to my plan; they returned within minutes. As they headed toward my cunning little trap I could feel my heart rate increase and the sweat begin to form on my palms. My shaking hand hovered over the rod; I dared not breathe. Closer and closer they came. I was fully expecting one of them to make a mistake, but it still shocked me when the rod hooped round and the line ripped from the spool. The battle was fraught, and at close quarters I could see and compensate for every move the fish made. The resulting 26 lb common put a huge smile on my face. I love it when a plan comes together!

I love it when a plan comes together.

It is good to get eyeball to eyeball with your targets.

That is just one exciting example of how effective stalking can be, and there are many more. To be totally honest with you, there are also many examples of when the whole thing has gone terribly wrong. However, it is those bad experiences that will teach you how to get it right in the future. Every situation will be different from the last, but messing up chances will still teach you something. And, as with everything in carp fishing, the more time you spend eyeball to eyeball with your target, the better you will become.

Stalking Tackle

Rod and Reel

In an age where most of the hype surrounding carp rods focuses on their ability to blast a lead way beyond the horizon, it is little wonder that anglers want to fish in that manner. After all, having paid out £200 or more on the latest mega-distance rod, most anglers would want to know that it works. There appears to be nothing subtle in carp fishing tackle these days: some of the rods and reels seem to be more suited to a tuna-fishing boat than the banks of a little carp lake. Now, don't get me wrong

here, I enjoy using all the latest gear too, and it has often been the case that I have had to use my longer-range equipment to take advantage of certain opportunistic situations, but I am always left feeling that the whole thing would have been made easier if I had been using gear more suited to the occasion.

For stalking in tight situations, 13 ft, horizon-casting rods are somewhat ungainly. For one, they are not forgiving enough when trying to deal with a fish at close range. Second, stalking, by its very nature, gets you into some really tight corners, where a long rod can be something of a liability. Therefore, I carry a 9 ft stalking rod. This length is ideal: I am not going to be casting very far with it and it is easier to manoeuvre in the undergrowth. With a test curve of $2^{1}/_{2}$ lb it will also be very forgiving at close quarters. I couple this with a small, but reliable, reel to balance the outfit.

Having had many opportunities to see carps' reaction to line, I am always conscious of trying to disguise it, or at the very least getting it hard on the bottom and out of harm's way. For some time now, I have been using a fluorocarbon main line. I have experimented with different breaking strains but found that the 12 lb version is ideal for this style of fishing. It sinks like a brick, and is practically invisible once in the water. It is also the toughest line I have ever used. Perfect for the job in hand!

Margin Rigs

And so to the business end of things. Many years ago, I could see no reason to use different rigs in the edge from those that I used in open water. After all, the fish picked them up out there, so why not in the edge? Time and experience have conspired to change my mind…as they nearly always do. Observation, again, has played a large part in my thinking. Carp are wild creatures and know instinctively that coming into the shallow margins to feed exposes them to danger. Not just because an angler may have set a trap there, but also because of the threat of predation. All this leads them to having their survival instincts on full alert. The slightest thing out of place could have them scurrying off, never to return. So what I now try to achieve with my end tackle is first, making the set-up as unobtrusive as possible and second, using any natural cover to hide it.

That said, I am not about to give you the definitive margin rig, because I don't believe there is one. What I intend to do is give you my ideas on rig construction, the materials I use and where, if possible, to place end tackle. Until I started using fluorocarbon main line I always used a leadcore leader. It didn't reflect sunlight, it was heavier than nylon so it couldn't waft up off the bottom when carp were in the area, and it was also tough enough to cope with the most extreme conditions. I still use it from time to time if snags are going to be a problem but, for most situations, the fluorocarbon is just fine. The lead attachment was the next thing I looked at. Lead clips seemed to be a little bulky and I worried that they might spook the carp. Out of necessity they need to be strong, and that strength comes from the bulk. In some situations they may be fine, but the more aware the carp are, the less likely I am to use them. For the most part I have taken to tying my leads on. This is done by using a two or three inch length of 2 lb breaking strain line to attach the lead to the hooklink swivel. By doing this I have taken out one item of tackle that could potentially alert the carp. In most stalking situations, I will be making a gentle underarm cast, so the lead will stay attached until a fish has been hooked. However, should the lead become snagged in any way during the fight, it can easily break free from the main line.

Much has been written about what size of lead to use. Generally, it makes sense to use a lead that is different from those that are normally being used on a water. For example, if everyone is using heavy leads, then try a much smaller one and see if you can trip the carp up. Having said that, I make no secret of the fact that, from choice, I like to use as heavy a lead as I possibly can. I find I am more confident and successful with heavy leads. At some stage, however, even when fishing in the edge, we are going to have to make a short cast and it is in this instance that I will use as light a lead as I can get away with. This is because, if there is no other choice but to cast to a spot, then I want to make as little disturbance as I can and, the lighter the lead, the less noise it will make on entry. This isn't an ideal situation for me, but if I spook the fish then I am never going to get a chance to hook one in the first place.

Running, or semi-fixed, is the next consideration. Again, I have much more confidence with a semi-fixed set-up. The shape of the lead is also very important to me. I like to use the flat-sided, dumpy style. These sit more flush to the bottom and they increase the bolt effect of my rigs. From what I have just said, it may seem that I always use a semi-fixed set-up, but that is not the case. Indeed, running leads in the margins accounted for two of my favourite carp captures (one of which I will use

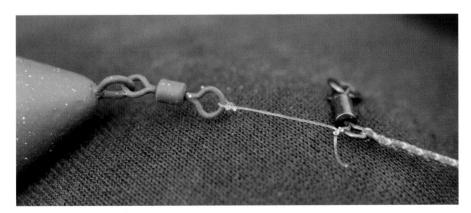

I have been tying my leads on…

at the end of this chapter to illustrate the points I am making). However, I do tend to use running leads only in very specific situations.

Hooklinks and Hooks

I simply love nylon hooklinks. Once again, fluorocarbon has helped to make life so much easier. I use it regularly for my margin hooklinks. Heavy, incredibly robust and almost invisible, it is ideal for the job. I am not a great lover of long hooklinks and usually keep them at about six to seven inches. Normally, I will form a D-rig and attach my bait via a braided hair on a rig ring. Of course, there are a thousand and one other materials to use. Much will depend on what you have the most confidence in. One problem I have come across is that many of today's modern strippable materials float and loop up off the bottom. This does not fill me with any great confidence. Of course, this situation is easily remedied by putting a small blob of rig putty on the hooklink. When stalking, however, the last thing I want to be doing is messing around with something like that. Thankfully, I have recently found one of these strippable materials that does sink, so I suspect it will be used a lot more. It also comes in various colours so I can match it to the bottom of the lake.

Fluorocarbon makes life so much easier.

A simple D-rig margin set-up.

Small hooks work…

In an effort to keep things as subtle as possible, I prefer to use as small a hook as I can. There is a theory that smaller hooks are not as strong as their bigger brethren, but I have not personally experienced problems with relatively small hooks. What I have noticed, in fact, is that more of a smaller hook penetrates the carp's mouth. And this, in turn, spreads the load over more of the hook. You will be surprised how small a hook you can use, even in the most fraught of conditions.

Hook Baits

Okay, so we have now got a very subtle rig, but what of the hook bait? The first question is: pop-up or bottom bait? I have caught carp on pop-ups in the edge, but by far the most effective presentation has been a bottom bait. Again, observation and experience have told me which one works best. These experiences have often left me wondering why I ever cast a pop-up out into open water, but I do, and I catch a lot of fish on them. In the edge though, the fish seem able to isolate and ignore that sort of presentation very easily. Therefore, I always use a bottom bait in the margins, making no attempt to give it any buoyancy at all. To match the baits I use for free offerings I invariably use half a boilie as a hook bait. As the old saying goes, 'it works for me'.

I have thought long and hard about baits for stalking.

Maggots mimic the carp's natural food.

Stalking baits are something that I have thought long and hard about. If I give you a couple of scenarios, I think you will see what I mean. First, you have crept up to the water's edge and discovered several fish feeding on a particular spot. They move off from time to time, but always return to feed. Do you risk introducing bait and alerting them to your presence, or should you just position a single hook bait? Second, you may have discovered carp swimming up and down a section of margin, but not feeding. Do you put bait in to try to get their attention, or once again introduce a single hook bait in the hope that they will pick it up out of curiosity? These really are some of life's little conundrums.

Personally, I like to see if I can get the fish to feed. I very rarely use just boilies to achieve this, relying instead on several other baits. Natural baits are without doubt among my favourites to use when stalking. Think about that for a second. How often do carp find little creepy-crawlies in the margin? Especially after heavy rainfall, all manner of creatures are washed into the edge and the fish will not be slow to capitalise on this. Maggots, casters and especially worms, mimic this situation and are often picked up without hesitation. They are instant and highly effective. A lot of the time though, we will not have these kinds of baits readily to hand. We sometimes have to make do with the bait that we have on the session. Response Pellets have been hugely successful for me, along with halved, quartered and crumbed boilies. Think about that combination for a second or two. How often do the carp see this kind of bait in the edge? Discarded hook baits that have been broken off the hair, plus spod spill, all help to keep the margins baited.

The trick at this point is not to introduce too much. I have found that lots of bait in the edge can often unsettle the carp, and of course putting it out creates a lot of disturbance. I normally use just a couple of handfuls at most.

Placement of End Tackle

The precise placement of the end tackle is crucial when stalking. Every effort must be made to keep it as unobtrusive as possible. Having found the spot on which the fish are feeding, try not to plonk the rig right in the centre of

I got it right on this occasion.

it. Instead, position the hook bait to one side; this will help minimise the amount of line and tackle the fish will come across. Maybe there is some weed on the bottom you can lay the line along; this is probably the best camouflage you can get. Remember that everything needs to be hard on the bottom and out of sight. The last thing we want is the line draping over weed up in the water, where the carp will pick it up on their fins.

One final point on this topic. You may well discover an area that the fish are frequenting, but be unable to induce a take. All is not lost, because it may be a spot that you can fish in a more static way. Let me give you an example that I believe encompasses all the factors that I have been discussing so far. The Car Park Lake at Yateley is, without doubt, the hardest lake I have fished. It contains only eight mirror carp and five or six smaller commons, and they are under intense pressure all year round. The lake is patrolled by some of the best margin fisherman I have ever come across. During my first season there, I watched for the first couple of weeks as one of these incredible chaps racked up an impressive number of fish in the margins of a small bay. All too soon, the carp got fed up with being caught and so he moved on to plunder another area. I kept my eye on this spot for a couple of days and soon discovered the carp were still cautiously visiting the area. I tried in vain to get a take by stalking in the daytime, but it was not to be. However, one particular spot seemed to be a favourite, so I baited it for several days in order for the fish to gain some confidence. I introduced small amounts of maggots, casters, Response Pellets, crumbed, chopped and whole boilies, just after dark. The area was no more than half a rod length out, and it was initially a small patch of sand surrounded by weed. By the time I was ready to fish it, because of the extra feeding activity the spot was twice its original size, and the far side extended to the marginal drop-off. This gave me the chance to use a rather large 5 oz running lead set-up. What I wanted was for the fish to pick up the hook bait, causing the lead to slide away into the deeper water – a situation I hoped they had not encountered before. After ensuring that the carp were not in the area, I waded gingerly to

the spot and placed the hook bait into position. Using the surrounding weed to cover the leadcore and main line, I slowly walked the rod back to the bank. To be honest, the spot looked somewhat comical. It seemed ridiculous that carp as large as 50 lb would be able to swim into two feet of water, but they did! My first customer was a fish called the Dustbin, at a little over 40 lb!

After a night at home, I returned for another overnight session. I set the trap in exactly the same way. At 4 a.m. I was once again called into action. The battle was lengthy and fraught, but eventually I was able to lead one more of my dream fish over the net cord. It was Single Scale at 43 lb 12 oz. Oh, deep joy!

All in all, the ideal place to fish.

In summary, it has often been said that fishing to features is one of the best ways of catching carp. Well, as I have said, the biggest feature on any lake, river or canal is the margin. Remarkably, this is the area that gets fished the least. Yet, in the early spring the marginal shallows will be the first area to warm up, and the carp will take advantage of this, especially since their natural food will be doing the same. Also, the margins are nearly always being pre-baited by anglers discarding leftover bait, so all in all, they are the ideal place to fish. Fishing the margins does takes a lot of patience, dexterity and hard work. The rewards, however, are just about as good as it gets!

13 OFF THE BOTTOM

It may surprise a great many anglers, but carp spend much of their time nowhere near the bottom of the lake. In the milder months, they will take advantage of the warmer upper layers and spend long periods simply basking in the sun. Weed beds, too, seem to hold a great attraction for them and they are very often to be found swimming around them in the hot weather. Snags and other overhead obstacles also hold their attention for long periods. If you are fortunate enough to be able to view fish in such places, you will notice that, although they look fairly dormant, they are simply finding and utilising places where they feel comfortable and safe.

In winter, their mid-water existence can be even more accentuated. Old wives' tales will tell you that, in the colder months, carp bury themselves in the deep silt that abounds in many of our lakes. Nothing could be further from the truth. The fact that many winter fish are caught with lots of leeches attached to them seems to lend more credence to that story, but I believe that those leeches have, for the most part, come from weed. The carp spend a great deal of time in weed in the winter because, since the water around it is a degree or two warmer than the rest of the venue, it is a comfortable place to be. In the absence of any great amount of weed, carp will be on the lookout for water layers that are slightly warmer than the rest of the lake. These are often referred

A 40 lb mirror feeding on the surface.

to as thermo-climes. Although, strictly speaking, they do not appear in water under 15 feet in depth, there are still warmer pockets in shallow water and carp will be quick to take advantage of them.

There is one other reason why I feel that carp spend a lot of time in the upper layers, and that is angling pressure. You will often hear anglers say that the carp can be found in the quieter parts of any venue. This gets them away from any lines and leads that are in the water. But what if the carp have no obvious safe haven to retreat to when the water is busy? The only way they can get away from the majority of the lines is by going to the centre of the lake and staying in the middle to upper layers.

Now, that may seem like doom and gloom: there seems to be a bit of a mental block for a lot of carp anglers when it comes to fishing in any other way but hard on the bottom. Since most of what is written about carp revolves around fishing on the bottom I suppose it is little wonder that some anglers believe it is the only way to catch carp. But this is wrong! There is a big leap of faith to take here because, believe it or not, at certain times you are far more likely to catch carp by fishing off the bottom. I'm emphasising the point about a leap of faith here because the ways I'm about to explain of presenting baits at various depths are not tactics that you should use for ten minutes and then discard when nothing has happened. Instead, these tactics should very often be used as your first line of attack.

Before looking at them in detail, I have a general point to make. Because we are trying to present baits off the bottom, this means that we will have to use slightly less robust tackle. Hooklinks will have to be a little more subtle, as will the size of the hook. In open water, this will not be a problem. However, if the venue is choked with weed or has an abundance of snags and lily beds, then you will have to think again. The last thing we should ever be doing is setting hooks in carp if we have no way of landing them. Please bear this in mind.

Zig-rigs

The zig-rig is a set-up in which the lead rests on the lake bed and a buoyant bait floats in the water above it at a depth determined by the length of the hooklink. This form of presentation is without doubt the hardest for most anglers to understand. Why the hell would a carp want to take a bait that was presented at mid water or at various other depths? Knowing that this will happen should be enough, but I like to know *why*. Unfortunately I cannot give a definitive answer, other than to say that much of what carp eat is, at some times, suspended in the water column. Water snails are a good example of this. But although carp may be used to finding the odd item of food here, I am sure the success of the presentation has much to do with curiosity. Let's put it this way, they have two options. They either swim around it or eat it.

When to use zig-rigs is the next question. On very heavily stocked waters I would say the answer is anytime. There will be a fair proportion of fish that are willing to feed on the bottom and, by the same token, there will probably be just as many cruising around in the upper layers. Thus there will always be a chance of a take on a bait fished way off the

A zig-rig just above the weed accounted for this magnificent mirror.

My biggest carp of 49 lb 4 oz fell to a zig-rig fished on the surface.

bottom. On venues with a lower stocking level we have to give this a little more thought. Carp are opportunist feeders; I have been fortunate to observe them in and around baited areas on many occasions. More often than not, they will dip down, only taking one or two mouthfuls, then swim off. While they are always up for a bit of free food, the difficulty here is that they are not feeding strongly enough to get caught. There will, of course, come a time when they start to feed on the bottom with confidence, and this is when the bottom-bait trap will be sprung. The more you fish a water, the more aware of these times you will become. If, for instance, you are getting bites on the bottom at mid-morning, then that is the time to be fishing there. But apart from getting those traps set at least an hour before I expect a bite, I will very often use the rest of the time to fish zig-rigs.

At what depth should you present the hook baits? Well, this is where you will need to employ a little trial and error. If the venue allows the use of three rods, then I would be looking to place hook baits at three different depths. In a water with an average depth of 10 feet, I would have baits at 2, 5 and 9 feet. If one of the rods starts to get action, then I will change the others to match. This increases your chances still further. The reason we cannot be too accurate to begin with is that it is very hard to ascertain at what depth the carp are swimming. Fishing different depths is the best way to find out.

I have been using zig-rigs a lot since the mid nineteen-nineties, and they have brought me some fantastic results. The first time I used them was to combat thick bottom weed, the idea being that I could present a bait just above the level of the weed and intercept the carp that way. This is still a valid tactic today. One other way to fish the rigs is to have the hook bait on the surface of the water. This surface/zig set-up accounted for my biggest-ever English carp; a capture that is recognised as the largest surface-caught carp of the twentieth century! This method is often referred to as just something to use on easy waters, but it is not. I could quote many examples of this working on some of the hardest lakes in the world. Have faith, it really does work.

Zig-rig Set-up

Let's start with the lead. To be honest, when I first used this rig I gave little consideration to the lead. I fished it with a running lead and thought that the heavier it was, the better it worked. The problem was that I would be using a long hooklink and, when playing a fish, the

Zig-rig lead

Zig-rig components.

heavy lead would swing around above the fish. The bigger it was, the more this problem accentuated itself. I tried lighter running leads but they were little better. Eventually, I started using light $1\frac{1}{2}$–2 oz in-line leads. Not only did they cut down on the amount of tangles, they also stayed connected to the hooklink swivel, and this helped tremendously.

Because, with this method, we have no way of disguising the hooklink, I have found it best to use the lightest that I can get away with. There is a nylon called Drennan Double Strength and this is the material that I use for all of my zig-rig fishing. The line is pre-stretched and because of this, the diameter is very low. It is quite a delicate line, but as long as you are not fishing in weed or snaggy areas it will cope very well. My friends often cringe when they see me fishing with this line because I have always tied it with a blood knot at the swivel end. Evidently, this is not the best knot to use with this material, but I have never had a problem with the line breaking at the knot. If you have any doubts then I would suggest you use a grinner knot to attach the swivel. I would hate you to blame me if you lost a fish or two!

I attach the hook with the 'no knot', with the tag end forming the hair. The first thing I do is strip off the required amount of line and tie a small loop at one end with an overhand knot. This is where the boilie stop will go. Attach the hook bait first, so that you can see exactly where it will end up in relation to the hook. I like it to sit on the bend of the hook, so the hair itself is going to be very short. Run the in-line lead up the main line and then connect the hooklink swivel to the end of this. Ensure that the swivel is housed in the front of the lead, and you are ready to go.

I find that it is best to use the smallest hook possible. Sizes 9, 10 and 11 are my favourites. Finally, I make a small groove in the hook bait and into that I push the bend of the hook, because this covers the hook slightly and makes the whole set-up a lot neater. Don't push the hook in too far, or you will lose much of the gape of the hook. This could lessen the chances of the hook finding a hold, especially when you consider the size being used!

The list of hook baits that can be used for this style of fishing is endless. It seems as if the only requirement of the bait is that it floats. There have even been stories of anglers cutting up old flip-flops and attaching bits of rubber to the hair, and catching! Personally, I have found a couple of favourite baits. For some reason, yellow is a highly attractive colour to carp: I have caught carp on a multitude of colours, but yellow definitely seems to be the best and plastic corn (maize) would usually be a good bet. Various plastic imitation baits all seem to find favour with carp anglers and my favourite by far is a plastic tiger nut. Don't ask me why, but when all else fails these usually get me out of jail. I also like to use heavily soaked pop-ups, but I never fish them in their round form, preferring to trim them down to make odd shapes. Whatever you choose to use, I suggest you make it small. Large baits tend to be treated with suspicion.

Casting and Playing Fish

Before we move on, I want to address the issue of casting out zig-rigs and landing fish. Using this method, I have caught carp on hook lengths as long as sixteen feet. The rods we use are normally 12–13 ft in length which, at times, is going to be way shorter than the hooklink. As you can appreciate, there are going to be problems with

A hook bait ready to go.

Plastic baits are a firm favourite.

Cut-down pop-ups work well.

Two different methods of hook bait attachment.

Landing a carp using a 14 ft hooklink.

this set-up both when casting and when you want to land fish.

Trying to cast in a confined swim could see you hooking up on all the foliage. I use an empty bucket that is positioned under the lead when it is held in the normal casting position. The hooklink is then placed in the bucket, and the cast is made. To ensure that no tangles occur, as the lead is about to hit the surface, trap the line on the spool with your finger. This ensures that the hook bait is thrown forward of the lead and will land with the hooklink fully extended.

Regarding landing a fish, if you have a friend or neighbouring angler to help this is not a problem, but on your own it can prove a little tricky. The rod will have to be held way back over your shoulder as you position the net. Take your time, steadily drawing the fish towards you. Any sudden movements could send the fish out into the lake again. Patience is your greatest ally here.

Surface Fishing

I have already talked about using the zig-rig to present a bait on the surface of the water, so I will not discuss that further here, except to make one point. The potential problem with doing this lies in the fact that the bait is anchored by a lead on the bottom of the lake. If there is little or no wind on the water, then that may not be too much of a worry. However, if there is a lot of water movement, then any free offerings you introduce are going to drift away from the hook bait. Not only does that draw the carp's attention away from the hook bait, it also alerts them to it because it does not behave naturally like the freebies. Therefore, if I am fishing zigs on the surface, I do not introduce any free offerings. Fishing this way is more suited to the static angler.

Feeding and catching carp off the top is, to me, one of the most awe-inspiring and exhilarating angling experiences. Not only can you see what you are fishing for – you can isolate individual fish and be a little more selective.

I keep my surface fishing gear completely separate from the rest of my equipment. This allows me to be very mobile and to gather up the gear I need at a moment's notice. Being mobile and organised means that I can react quickly to any opportunities that may arise. Very often in the warmer months – when you are most likely to catch fish this way – I spend the whole day at a water constantly on the move.

Surface Rod

A balanced surface fishing set-up.

I use this braid for all my surface fishing.

Floating braid keeps you in direct contact.

Although I have caught carp off the top on my standard rods, it is far better to use one that has been purpose-made for the task. Remember that you will be using relatively light line and hooklinks. A powerful rod is not best suited to dealing with that kind of tackle. My controller rod is 12 ft in length and has a test curve of $2^{1}/_{4}$ lb. Its soft action helps tremendously to cushion the lunges of a carp on a short line. The outfit is balanced, and helps to make the whole experience a lot more exciting.

Reel

Because you are using a light rod it makes sense to use a reel that balances this. There is little point in using a reel designed for big pit fishing; it will just be cumbersome and a hindrance. A small free-spool reel is all that you need. The Stratos reels that I use have fantastic line lay and this helps when casting lighter weights. The clutch is also very smooth and this comes into its own when a fish has been hooked. Ensure that the reel you use is the best you can afford. There is little margin for error when fishing on the top.

Line

For many years I was quite happy using a good quality monofilament in either 10 or 12 lb breaking strain. However, things have now moved on a little. Nylon makes it very difficult for the angler to stay in direct contact with either the hook bait or the controller float that may be on the line. The bow created by water movement and wind is far greater with nylon than with any of the modern floating braids. Therefore, floating braid is what I use for all my surface fishing. Anyone who has ever been float fishing will know how important it is to stay in direct contact with the float. This enables the angler to react and strike bites instantly. Braid does not seem to suffer so much as nylon from water movement or wind and this, and its lack of stretch, helps in hitting even the most finicky of takes. The fact that braid floats also helps in 'mending' the line if it does bow. This, again, keeps you in direct contact. The 14 lb braid that I use has the diameter of 6 lb nylon line, so casting is not a problem. Playing fish on braid can be a little scary, but when it is used with the light rod there shouldn't be a problem. However, with no stretch in the braid it is very important to have the reel's clutch set properly. The fragile nature of the hooklink will not stand too much punishment.

End Tackle

In its purest form, surface fishing is done with a free-lined bait. This is simply a hook tied on the end of the line, onto which the hook bait is attached. Nothing else is put on the line. This is the way that I prefer to catch carp off the top. Unfortunately, in today's pressured carp fishing environment this situation rarely arises. More often than not, the fish will be a little further out than the margins, and this will mean that the angler has to add casting weight to the line in order to reach them. The floats used for this are called controllers. They come in various shapes and sizes and are selected according to

Controller and bubble floats.

A rubber float stop gives something of a bolt effect.

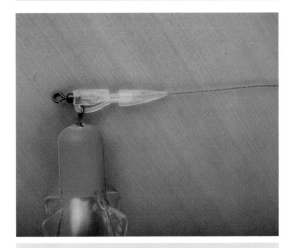

A tiny lead clip is a brilliant alternative method of attaching a controller.

the distance you want to cast. In the traditional designs, at the top of the float there will be a swivel and this is what the main line is run through. Below the swivel there will be a highly visible sight bob, so the controller is a good indicator of where your hook bait is at range. At the base there will be a weight, which helps with the casting, and cocks the float once cast out. It is always worth remembering that, on the surface, carp will feel exposed and be on full alert, so always use the smallest controller you can get away with. A large object crashing into the water is a sure-fire way of frightening them off and, even with a smaller controller, it is always best to cast beyond and/or upwind of the fish and work the rig slowly back into position.

Another characteristic of these floats is that they tend to be very long in the body and sit deep in the water. Observation and experience have taught me that the carp very often suss this out, and this helps them to identify the hook bait. Sometimes, they refuse to feed in the area of the float at all. Therefore, for the last couple of years I have been using bubble floats. Basically, these are small, round, clear plastic orbs that can be filled with water to get the required casting distance. The unobtrusive nature of bubble floats, and the fact that they sit high in the water, has made them an invaluable addition to my surface armoury.

To attach these floatation devices to the line, simply thread a small rubber float stop up the main line. Then, for a standard controller, run the line through the swivel or, in the case of a bubble float, through the central holes provided. Attach the hooklink swivel and we are nearly done. The rubber float stop is there to stop the controller flying back up the line and gives something of a bolt effect to the set-up.

Alternatively, you can use a tiny lead clip device. This is a great way to set up for surface fishing. Not only does it allow you to change the controller quickly, it also means that, should the controller get caught up in weed, it can be released from the line.

Hooklink

The choice of hooklink material is one of the most important aspects to consider. As with zig-rig fishing, I use the Double Strength line exclusively. Spools of 8, 10 and 12 lb line cover just about every situation and its thin diameter makes it hard for the fish to detect. A word of warning here: although fluorocarbon lines are almost impossible for the fish to see, they are absolutely no use in this situation. Unfortunately, they sink very quickly and this will ruin your presentation.

The hooklink itself will need to be at least 3 ft in length: my preference is for one of 5–6 ft. This ensures the hook bait is a sensible distance away from the controller.

Hooking Arrangements and Hook Bait Attachment

When fishing on the surface, there is a need to make the hook as inconspicuous as possible. To that end, as with the zigs, I use as small a hook as I can get away with. Not only does this make it hard for the carp to see, it will affect the buoyancy of the hook bait less. (Bread is a very obvious surface bait, and with this you will be able to use a bigger hook because you will be burying the hook in it. With the more standard surface baits such as Chum Mixers, you will have to be more careful.)

There are several ways in which we can attach the hook bait to the hook, and the method chosen will depend in part on the bait being used, which I will discuss next. When using classic surface baits such as mixer biscuits, by making a small groove in the hook bait it can then be super-glued to the hook shank. Another option is to use a rubber bait band.

If it floats it can be used as a surface bait.

Glue, bait band or hair – the choice is yours.

This is threaded onto the shank, and the bait held in position by the band. The way I like to fish on the surface is by using a very short hair. This leaves the whole of the hook exposed and makes hooking easier. If you are going to hair rig a mixer or similar bait you will need to use a nut drill to make the hole. If you attempt to push a baiting needle through a mixer it will split.

Surface Baits

Basically, if it floats, it can be used as a surface bait. Many anglers have started to use a variety of plastic imitations. While these have the advantage that there is little need to keep changing the hook bait, I have found that some patterns are far too buoyant. This buoyancy makes it easy for the carp to isolate the hook bait and, in all but the most competitive of feeding situations, it will be ignored. That said, there are now imitation mixers available that carry a small shot in their base. This helps to take away some of buoyancy and these have proved to be very effective.

The most famous surface bait has to be the Chum Mixer. Unfortunately, the company has changed the recipe and they are no longer as buoyant as they used to be. Many of the large supermarket stores have their own variety of pet mixer biscuits and I have discovered that many of these are just fine for the job. In fact, there are any number of pet foods that can be used. Many of the cat biscuits are great because they come in different sizes. However, please ensure that your chosen brand floats before you take them onto the bank.

Although some people use these mixers doubled up, I believe that a double hook bait is too obvious and prefer to use a single one on a hair. Just make sure that you have plenty drilled out beforehand because you will have to change the hook bait quite frequently.

To my mind, pet food biscuits are best fished as they come out of the packet, but some anglers prefer to flavour them and this can be done by simply spraying the desired flavour over the bait and shaking it up in a plastic bag.

Floating trout pellets are another great surface bait. After all, trout

pellets are used a hell of a lot for fishing on the bottom, so why not on the top? They are also available in a variety of sizes, which helps to confuse the carp when they are trying to isolate the hook bait.

Pop-up boilies make excellent surface baits, but I never use them in their normal round state. Instead, I cut them down to mimic the free offerings I am using.

As I said, the list of potential surface baits is endless. Various seeds, such as sunflower seeds, float, as do some sweets. I have had success with Maltesers. Some anglers have had a great deal of success by making up a buoyant boilie mix. I have never made this kind of bait, so have no

Chum Mixers led to the capture of this summer common.

Drill some mixers ready to use as hook baits.

experience of it, but it is another avenue to explore. Once again, we are limited only by our imagination. Get out to the local shops and have a look. You just might find something new that the carp are prepared to eat.

Free Offerings and Casting

While I have had limited success casting a single mixer to carp, by far the best way is to get them feeding first. The main thing here is to take your time. The more competition you can create, the more likely they are to make a mistake with the hook bait. The first thing to do when you have found a group of fish on the surface, is to see if it is possible to drift the free offerings in towards the fish. The last thing you want to do is to spray them all over their heads! The best way to introduce them is upwind of the fish so that they drift towards the carp. Sometimes the fish will display no interest whatsoever, no matter how long you try. In this case you will have to find some other fish that may be a bit more co-operative. A lot of the time though, there will be at least some interest. Don't go mad at this stage; use just enough freebies to maintain their interest. Only increase the amount of free offerings once the fish begin

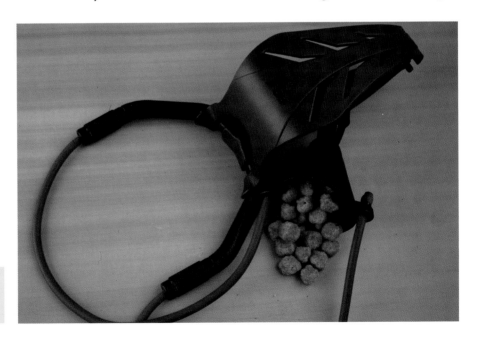

Using free offerings.

Using a stone in a PVA bag is a great way of introducing mixers at range.

to feed in earnest. Between each catapult load of bait, you should be getting your rod ready to cast. If you have taken your time and fed them correctly, then all of a sudden they will be charging around trying to find every last one of your baits. Now is the time to make a cast.

By now, your fingers will have become like ten Cumberland sausages, and you will be shaking like a leaf. Take a deep breath and try to stay calm. A mistake here, and all your efforts will have been for nothing. As with the free offerings, the last thing you want to do is cast directly at the carp. If there is a wind blowing, then cast the hook bait to the upwind side of the fish and let it drift in towards them. If there is no wind, then you will have to cast far beyond them and slowly inch the hook bait back until it is amongst the fish. If they are still competing there is every chance of an immediate take and you must be prepared for this. In the meantime, keep feeding the free offerings to maintain the feeding response. The trick here is not to cast too often. It is a mistake all of us can make and sometimes it is hard not to do so. Bite the bullet, and even if the bait has drifted away from the fish, leave it for a while. Sometimes this tricks the odd carp that may not be feeding amongst the main shoal. Above all, keep the bait going in. I have lost count of the number of times I have had a take and the rest have continued to feed.

Getting the rod back into action as quickly as possible after landing a fish is important, because you could go on to catch three or even four of the fish before the commotion eventually scares them off. Being organised and having everything to hand is essential if you are to make the most of this incredibly exciting branch of carp angling.

14 PLAYING, LANDING AND HANDLING

Playing an angry carp can be the most exhilarating experience. I would even go so far as to say that it can be downright frightening at times. It is the culmination of all the hard work and sacrifice that we have been through. From the second the alarm lets out its shrill call, your heart will be in your mouth, the old knees will start to tremble and all you will be thinking about is getting the fish into the bottom of your landing net. This, however, is the moment that we are all waiting for. Not until the fight is over can we appreciate how spectacular it has been. If you have yet to feel the immense power of a hooked carp then I envy you this first experience. It is the moment that will probably hook you on carp fishing for life.

The carp know every trick in the book. Not only are they trying to pull your arms out of their sockets, they are also looking for ways to escape. Being much more aware of their environment than we are, they know where all the snags, weed beds and other underwater obstacles are. It is these that they are trying to reach, in an effort to shed the hook. The angler on the bank has to be ready for this and able to compensate for any changes in direction or sudden bursts of speed. These abilities ensure that the fish is landed and, most importantly of all, is not left towing tackle because it has been able to reach one of its sanctuaries. The carp's welfare should always be uppermost in our minds!

One thing that has become obvious over the years is that the fight from a smaller carp, say up to 20 lb, is a lot different from one that is 30 lb plus. Smaller carp can generate more speed a lot more quickly than their bigger brethren. The fight from such a fish will involve short bursts, punctuated with lots of head-shaking that will cause the rod tip to bounce a lot. Larger carp will be much more powerful, but tend to be slower and more deliberate. Don't be fooled into thinking that these will be easier to land – they won't! Their powerful runs are hard to stop, and only by the use of steady pressure will you be able to gain control.

Carp have very soft mouths and this means that if we do not allow the fish to run at times, there is a danger that the hook may be pulled out. In open water this need to let them run may not cause problems but, when faced with underwater obstacles, more pressure will need to be applied. My advice would be to target smaller fish until you have mastered all the skills needed to deal with bigger fish. It's a

Your heart will be in your mouth…

The carp know every trick in the book.

Patience is a virtue.

massive cliché, I know, but it is best to learn to walk before you can run.

Open Water

Let's take a look first at what would be considered the easiest conditions in which to land a carp – an open lake with no snags or weed. On this type of venue it is not necessary to have the rods set up in any special way, and we can allow a taking carp to strip line from a fairly loose clutch or free-spool facility. In saying that, I still like fairly heavy tension on the reel. This ensures that the carp has to work hard to take line and I am in control from the moment I pick up the rod. There really is little need to strike in the conventional way, as the lead and the hook will have done their job and the fish will be well hooked. What I do is to tighten into the fish and keep as heavy pressure on it as I dare, until the fish dictates what action I need to take next. Very often, the initial pressure will stop the fish running, but now and again the rod will nearly be torn from your grasp. When this happens, let it run, but increase the pressure steadily and eventually it will stop and change direction. It is difficult to be definite about what exactly will happen, because all fish behave differently, but this is a general guideline. Above all, take your time, enjoy the fight and be patient – it really is a virtue when playing a carp.

Weed

Increasingly these days, possibly through the effects of global warming and climate change, we are faced with weedy water. From the carp's perspective this can only be a good thing. Weed is one of nature's natural filters and helps to maintain the quality of the water. The better the quality, the more the carp will thrive, and so will their natural food items. Weed is an

The weed-infested Conningbrook produced this immaculate 28 lb common.

absolute haven for many of the things that carp feed on naturally. On most waters it is possible to find carp in and around these weedy areas. This is because during the daylight hours, weed is producing oxygen through the process of photosynthesis. This makes it a very comfortable place for the fish to be. At night, however, the weed produces carbon dioxide, which forces the natural food out into the open water, and the carp of course follow it. However, small creatures such as snails won't go too far from the weed and a bait presented near it is very likely to be taken. The danger is that a hooked fish will head straight back into it once it knows it has made a mistake. It is now that we need to be more aware about what is happening. Light weed may not cause too much of a problem, but big beds of heavy weed can often result in a lost fish.

Again, I can only talk about the tactics that I use in this situation, but they have stood me in good stead for many years. First, when a take occurs, I want the carp to take as little line as possible from the reel. To that end, I tighten up the free-spool or clutch so that it is very hard for the carp to run. This, in turn, means that due consideration must be given to tackle and its basic set-up. When fishing in open water you have the opportunity to use tackle that is fairly light. With no dangerous obstacles to overcome, you can get away with gear that is suited to the size of the carp that you intend to catch. Fishing near weed, on the other hand, presents a whole different ball game. For those who are not familiar with weed (and without going into the specific varieties), I can

In weed your tackle needs to be up to the job.

Weed can be a help and a hindrance.

tell you it can be a very abrasive substance. The shells of natural food such as mussels and snails only add to this problem. Therefore, a main line of 15 lb is the minimum I would use. Couple that with a leadcore leader or rig tubing to further enhance the durability of the last few feet of your line, and you should be okay. Remember, though, that during the fight the line may get an awful lot of weed wrapped around it and your tackle needs to be up to the task. Not only are we trying to avoid tears at our end but, more importantly, we don't want to leave the fish trailing with lost tackle.

Because the aim is not to give the fish much line on the take, rod set-up is crucial. The last thing you want to happen is for the rod to be dragged into the water. I like to use single bank sticks in this situation, and I never point the rod directly at the baited area. This allows the rod to act as something of a shock absorber and soak up some of the power of a taking fish. Ensure that the rear butt rest is able to grip the rod and also ensure that the butt ring of the rod is to the inside of the bite alarm. You will also need to stay near your rod at all times to react quickly to a take. This ensures that you have immediate control and, as much as it may not seem like it at times, you can dictate proceedings to the carp in the main.

With this set-up and response hopefully, if the carp does reach the weed, it will not be able to bury itself too far into it. The less weed there is on the line, the easier it will be to extract the carp. On many occasions, if sufficient pressure is applied, the carp, knowing that it can't run into the weedy sanctuary, will veer away from the obstacle and this makes life so much easier. That said, during the fight it will still try to get its head into any other bits of weed that it can find. This will test your courage to the limit, as you simply have to keep the pressure on and not allow it to bury itself. Keep the fish moving. Sometimes the carp will pick up weed on the line and this will cover its eyes so that it can't see where it is going, which means that you can simply reel it to the net – but don't bank on this happening.

At some stage, despite your best efforts, you are going to be faced with a fish that has gone so far into weed that you are simply unable to budge it. I have

Being near to the rods means that you have immediate control.

seen many anglers, when faced with this situation, simply point the rod at the fish and walk backwards. This is called 'pulling for a break' and it is the last thing you need to be doing…literally! The first thing I do is release the bale arm on the reel and leave the line completely slack. The rod is then placed back onto the rest and the bale arm is closed, the alarm is switched on and the free-spool facility engaged. I will then wait five or ten minutes to see if the fish will move. Very often at this stage, the quick release of pressure suggests to the fish that it has got away and it will move off. As soon as you see or hear any movement, pick up the rod and once again get the fish on the move. This method has worked more often than not. If it does not, I then tighten up to the fish and leave the rod in the rest under a lot of compression. The constant pressure sometimes gets them on the move. I alternate between the two methods for anything up to two or three hours. Eventually, I am afraid, the only way to sort things out is to point the rod at the area and walk slowly backwards. It's not the best way to sort things out, but other than cutting the line it's all that's left. After a lengthy period I will be pretty sure that the fish has shed the hook, and hopefully all I will be doing is pulling in a load of weed. Be careful though, because now and again the fish will still be there and you will have to scoop it into the net, weed and all.

One thing I have found to be a definite advantage when fishing in weedy areas is to use a lead clip. With the lead ejected from the main line, it makes it so much easier to get the fish moving. The lead, if it remains attached, will gather more weed than any other item of tackle. It is not an exact science; all I would ask is that you think about the well-being of the carp.

Lead clips are a definite advantage in weed.

Snags

In this section I would also include areas of water lilies. These are not spots for the faint-hearted or inexperienced angler to fish. I hope that doesn't sound condescending because it is not meant to be. It is simply that they are the most difficult places to fish and to extract carp from safely. The problem is that carp love to be in these sorts of areas, sometimes spending days, even weeks, holed up in one particular spot. If you have done your homework and walked the lake before committing to a particular swim, then you may well find them there. But if you are unsure how to target them or lack the experience necessary to extract them, then please leave them be. There is little point in hooking a carp only to lose it, and in all honesty those that continue to do this have no right to be fishing for carp in the first place!

I remember having a conversation with a local tackle shop owner. A young lad had been dropped off at a lake by his father. Having read an article in which the author said he fished in snags, the young boy decided this was the thing to do. The father came into the shop the next morning and said that his son had lost eleven fish! Alarms bells started to ring and the tackle shop owner, helpful as ever, decided to go along and

Fishing locked up to snags – and near the rods.

see what the problem was. He was mortified to see that the young lad was casting over a fallen tree into the thickest snags on the lake. Little wonder then, that the carp were breaking his main line! I always think that anything written about snag fishing should start with the statement that we are fishing *to* the snags, not *in* them.

It is not just a case of casting to a fallen tree, either. Often what we can see above water level is the tip of the iceberg, so every effort should be made to discover what lies beneath the water as well. This will tell you how close to the snags you can present a hook bait, and what problems you will encounter once a fish has been hooked.

The important thing here is that, once the hook bait is in position, the carp cannot get any line from your reel if it makes a mistake. This is called fishing 'locked up'. The first thing necessary is to take a close look at the rod set-up. Mine is much the same as I would use for fishing in weed. The only difference with snag fishing is that I point the rod at the area in which the hook bait is lying. This is because even the bending of the rod could be enough for the carp to get back into the snags and, much as I dislike using tight lines this is the only way to ensure the carp can gain no momentum. Once again the butt ring must be inside the

alarm, and a gripper style rear rest used to secure the butt of the rod. You will also be fishing for single bleeps from the alarm, so it is vital that you use it on its most sensitive setting.

For this style of fishing, never stray far from your rods and by that I mean no more than a couple of yards. You have to react instantly to any indication. The same is true if you intend to fish to the snags during the night. You must sleep as close as possible to your rods. This is something I don't like doing, and many has been the time when I have moved the snag rod into open water. I would rather not hook a carp at all, than risk leaving tackle in it. Worse still is the thought of the fish ending up tethered to the snag. I know I keep on labouring this point but I make no apology. The carp's welfare must come first.

Once you have got an indication, get control of the rod as quickly as possible. This is the time in carp fishing where your bravery will be tested to its absolute limits. You cannot afford to give the fish even an inch of line. With the reel locked up there is no need to, so I simply walk slowly backwards. Because the carp hasn't been able to get up a head of steam, it is surprising how easy this can be. Don't release the pressure until you are sure you have got the fish well away from any danger. Remember

> Don't release the pressure until the carp is in open water.

A 32 lb mirror being returned next to the snag that it was caught from.

Any mistake now and the carp will make good its escape.

that probably the first thing a hooked fish will do is head straight back to the snag from which you have hooked him. Once in open water you will be able to play the fish normally and lead him toward the waiting net.

Landing Fish

While a fish is being played in open water, the cushioning effect of the rod and the line (if using monofilament) may well cover up any heavy-handedness on our part. As the fish nears the net, however, these cushioning effects will be drastically reduced. Any mistakes now may result in the lead and end tackle whistling past your ear as the fish makes good its escape. Taking your time now will really pay dividends. To

begin with, you are drawing the fish into an area where it will feel vulnerable and it will make every attempt to get back into deep water. Then the landing net itself will undoubtedly unnerve the fish, and it will be trying to get as far away from that as possible. Expect the carp to do the unexpected and be ready to compensate for it.

Initially, what you are trying to do is to get the carp's head on the surface. Usually, once it has had a couple of gulps of air it can be led towards the net. Try to keep a long line on the fish, and by that I mean from the rod tip to the carp. I normally try to leave about a rod's length as I draw the fish over the net cord. This is usually enough to compensate for any last-minute lunges. At this stage you are trying to draw as much of the fish as possible over the net. If you attempt to raise the mesh too soon, you will be in danger of frightening the carp and making it bolt out of netting range. With smaller fish this may not be too much of a problem, but the bigger they are, the more careful you will have to be.

Don't raise the mesh too early.

Get the carp's head near to the spreader block of the landing net and there shouldn't be too many problems. Since, as I said earlier, the landing net may well frighten the fish, I have found it best not to chase them around with it. Set it down in the position from which you want to land the fish and draw the fish towards it. If you have a friend on hand to do the netting for you, then so much the better. I would, however, remind him that *you* will lead the fish to *him*.

Once the carp is over the net, simply lift the mesh around the fish and ensure that it comes to rest in the bottom of the net. Check that nothing, such as the hook or any other end tackle, has got caught in the mesh. This could potentially cause the fish damage, the last thing we want to do. If you are anything like me, you will then let out a huge sigh of relief and take a moment or two to regain your composure. You have just done what you set out to do. Wonderful!

Landing fish at night can cause a few problems. For the record, I have never used a head torch to land a fish, unless of course there has been a very good reason to do so. I worry that the light will further frighten the fish, and that can cause it to bolt once again. It's a bit of a catch-22 really;

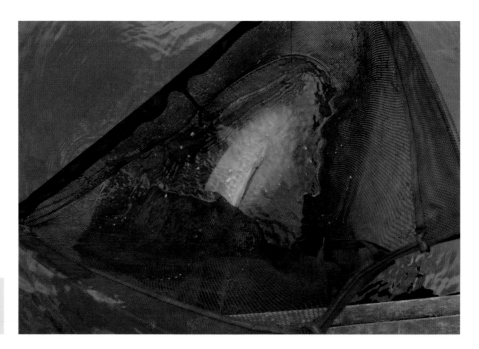

Got him!
This is where we want them to end up.

if you lack the experience or confidence to do without, then you are going to have to use one. If you intend to do so, my suggestion would be to have the head torch switched on as soon as battle commences. Then, at the very least, when the carp does come into netting range the light will already be on the water. I am sure this will be less frightening than switching it on just as the fish is about to go in the landing net.

The main things to remember when landing a carp are to take your time, don't stab at the fish with the net, and ensure that it is fully over the net cord before you lift the net around it.

Handling

A carp on the bank is a carp at its most susceptible to harm. We have removed it from its natural environment and every care must be taken to ensure that we return it to the water in the same condition that we took

We must take every care...

it out. Apart from primary consideration for the fish, you may just have landed the carp of your dreams and it will be the source of other anglers' dreams. Returning it in perfect condition will mean that any subsequent captures aren't tainted by any damage.

Carp are very hardy creatures and can survive in the most adverse conditions. There are examples of carp living for forty or fifty years, surviving numerous captures every season. However, it is only through careful handling on the bank that their longevity has been assured. In the warmer months you will undoubtedly witness carp spawning. During this annual event, their instinctive drive to procreate will cause incredible damage to the fish. Scales will be ripped from their flanks and very often large cuts will appear. They recover well from this because it is a natural process. The stress of capture however, could lessen their ability to recover if we damage them.

Be Organised

Long before a carp has come to rest in the bottom of the landing net, things must be in place ready to receive any fish we are lucky enough to catch. The first thing I do when I arrive in the selected swim is to set up my landing net. This, to be honest, is a habit that was born out of superstition, but on the odd occasion when I have had an immediate take, it has saved the day. The last thing you want to be doing is messing around setting up the net whilst an angry carp is careering around the lake. On more prolific venues, I have taken to using two landing nets. While I am sure that two carp in the same net will come to little harm, it puts my mind at rest if they are cocooned in different nets.

On prolific venues I have taken to using two nets.

Having sorted out your landing net, don't set up your bivvy too far from your rods. Not only will you be in contravention of Environment Agency laws, you will also be unable to react quickly to any indication you may get.

The next thing to look at is what I call a reception area for the carp. This is the area where you will set out your unhooking mat. Gone are the days when anglers placed their fish on the nearest piece of grass, thankfully. However, I still see anglers with thousands of pounds worth of tackle on the bank, yet with a mat that is woefully inadequate. Most true anglers will be more impressed by the fact that you intend to look after the fish than by any amount of expensive tackle. Basically, the larger and more padded the mat is, the better. Look for a soft area to place it on. Natural hollows in the ground make ideal spots, as they help to cushion the fish even more. Obviously, there will be occasions when there will be no grass in the area. In such an instance I would seek the help of a friend or neighbouring angler. Their unhooking mat will add to the protection. I have, in the past, used my sleeping bag to ensure that no harm comes to the carp. Extreme, I will admit, but necessary at times!

Once you have selected an area for the mat, the next thing to ensure is that all the necessary equipment is at hand to deal with a landed carp. Weigh sling, scales, first aid kit and, if necessary, a carp sack. This last I will deal with shortly, but it is essential to have all these items to hand. There is nothing worse than having a lively carp on the mat while you are having to search around in the back of your bivvy for the relevant kit! With everything to hand, life for you and the carp will be so much easier.

Being organised is fundamental to looking after the carp.

Make sure that the mat has been wetted thoroughly.

Collapse the net and roll it down to the carp, ensuring that its fins are lying naturally along its body.

From Net to Mat

With the carp safely in the bottom of the net, the next thing is to transfer it to the unhooking mat. Before any fish is placed on the mat, make sure that it has been thoroughly wetted. They tend to get very hot on summer days! It is a good idea also to wet the weigh sling at this stage, especially if you are on your own.

Make sure that the pressure is released from the hook by stripping a few yards of line off the reel and laying it in the bottom of the net with the fish. So that the fish cannot flap around in the net, collapse it and roll it down to the carp. You aren't trying to totally wrap the fish up, just restrict its movement. Please ensure that you check that the fins are lying naturally along its body, and none of the dorsal fin rays are sticking through the mesh. Once you are happy that the carp will come to no harm, you can then lift it from the water. Whilst transferring it to the mat, hold it as near to the ground as possible. In the event that you lose your footing or slip, the fish will not fall too far. Next, place the carp gently on the mat. I see an awful lot of anglers at this stage remaining standing and simply bending over the mat. You will have little or no control of the fish if you do it this way. Instead, kneel down low over the fish; this will allow you to react to any flapping around that may occur. So what, if you knees get a little muddy or wet?

At this point we are all eager to have a good look at our prize, but first of all the hook will need to be removed. Try to keep as much of the fish as possible (especially the eyes) covered by the mesh, as this will help to keep it calm. Push the hook back the way it went in. Most hooks are armed with micro-barbs and they will come out very easily. I have never had the need to use forceps or any other unhooking device. The beauty of the hair rig means that carp are not often deeply hooked. In saying that, I always keep a pair of pliers handy. The reason for this is that, very rarely, a hook may turn back in on itself and double-hook the fish. This is something that can happen with any pattern of hook, regardless of its shape or size!

If this happens, please make no attempt to extract the hook by conventional means, as this may lead to damage. Instead, thread the hook right through until the barb is fully exposed. Then, using the pliers, cut the hook point off below the barb and thread the hook out of the carp's mouth. Yes, you will be sacrificing a hook, and will have to tie a new hooklink, but this is a very small price to pay when you consider the well-being of the carp.

Now is the time to put on any carp-care medication that may be necessary. Personally, I use Orabase, which can be bought from most chemists. It is a little expensive, but I believe it is the best that I have used. Then you can take a moment or two to admire the fish. While you are doing so, check it out for any other damage. Many carp seem susceptible to small sores, especially after spawning, and these should also be treated with Orabase.

Weighing

The first thing to be done is to zero the scales. I use digital scales all the time now, as these are so easy to zero; all it involves is hanging the weigh sling from the hook at the bottom of the scales. Then, holding the scales by the handles, all I need to do is press one

Push the hook back the way it went in.

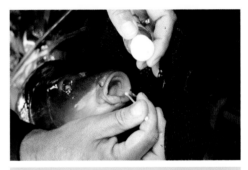

Now is the time to put on any carp-care medication.

The first thing to be done is to zero the scales.

Slip the carp gently into the weigh sling.

Always hold the scales by the handles or ring provided.

button and the scales will read zero. This is essential for accurate weighing. Dial scales will need to be adjusted manually by tweaking the little disc adjuster situated at the top of the scales. Once this has been done, take the sling off and lay it down next to the fish. There is no need to lift the fish off the ground at this stage, simply slip it into the sling. Once again, check that the fins are lying flush against the body. Put the cord of the sling back onto the hook of the scales and steadily raise it up until all of the fish is off the ground. It will take a second or two for the fish to settle, and then an accurate reading can be taken. One word of warning: always hold the scales by the handles or the ring provided. If you cup the scales around the main body you will get a false reading. It makes the fish weigh more, believe it or not. While that may make you feel good in the short term, you are only lying to yourself! Some cheats in carp fishing have prospered, I'm afraid, but they have little or no respect from other anglers. Weigh the fish properly and be honest – it really is the best policy!

Photography

I guess it is fair to say that the vast majority of us want some kind of permanent record of our catches. It goes without saying that the better quality your camera is, the better the shots will be. The problem here is that, no matter how good the camera, it is all dependent on the person using it at the time. If you are fishing with a friend who knows how to take pictures then the problems won't be so bad. It is when you get someone unknown from further up the bank, or a passer-by, that things can go wrong. I have lost count of the number of bad pictures I have had taken by people who didn't know one end of a camera from the other. This is why I believe

One hand goes under the head …

… and the other under the anal fin.

that digital cameras are one of the greatest carp-care instruments ever made. Gone are the days of taking a whole roll of film just in the hope that one of the pictures will be 'the one'. Digital cameras allow the user to see the results of the work immediately. This means that adjustments can be made with the minimum of fuss and stress to the carp. If you don't own one, then I suggest you make it your first priority if you want quality shots of your latest capture. I always keep my camera handy so that anyone will be able to pick it up and use it.

So, with the weighing completed, the carp should be gently lowered to the mat once again. Keep the fish inside the weigh sling while you instruct the photographer about what to do. Once both captor and photographer are happy, the pictures can be taken. Slip your hands gently inside the weigh sling and place one hand under the carp's head. The ideal point is where the pectoral fins are, just under the gill covers. The other hand should be positioned around the anal fin. The carp will be well balanced now, and you can gently lift it off the mat. Remain on your knees and never try to stand up. If you do so, and the carp flips, you will have no control, and if it falls from such a height then damage will be inevitable.

Hold the fish low over the mat while the pictures are taken. If you want any different angles, then instruct the photographer to move. You should remain still and in control of the fish at all times. Inevitably, there

A container of lake water helps to keep the fish wet.

A perfect shot of a perfect carp.

will be times when the fish is going to be lively. By having it low you can cushion its descent back to the mat. Cover its eyes with the net or weigh sling and wait for it to settle down again. From experience, it is best to be firm but gentle with the fish. It is almost as if it realises you are nervous and tries to take advantage. Only as you hold more and more fish will this process become easier.

There is no need for the fish to be out of the water for more than three or four minutes at most. Even for that short period, it is always best to have a container on hand with some lake water in it. This can be used to keep the fish wet and it will look a lot better in the pictures. With everything in position and organised, you will be able to get the fish back in the water a lot quicker.

Sacking

Because of its misuse, sacking of carp has been banned on many waters, and with very good cause. Even after nearly thirty years of carp fishing experience, I get extremely nervous if I have to retain a carp for any length of time in a sack. To be quite frank with you, there is little or no need to do this anymore, because modern cameras are so good at taking flash photography. Most also have the facilities for the captor to get self-taken shots, an area I am trying to come to terms with as I write. However, there may come a time when you will want to sack a fish so that you can go and recruit a photographer or wait for a friend to arrive. For very short periods, the fish will be fine if held in the landing net. The problem here is if you are fishing the windward bank and the water is shallow, in which case there is a very great danger of the fish getting damaged. In such a situation, for any period longer than five or ten minutes, I would place the fish in a sack. This allows the carp to find a depth at which it is comfortable. However, I have heard horror stories of carp being retained for fourteen or fifteen hours. This is totally unacceptable: they should be retained for the minimum amount of time possible, and I would think an hour or two would be the absolute maximum.

If you think it may be necessary to use a sack then, once again, it should be close at hand to avoid the carp being left unattended. First and foremost, it must be big enough to house the fish you want to retain. This allows for maximum water flow through the mesh. The sack should then be thoroughly soaked. Place it open, next to the fish, and gently ease the fish into it. Zip it up or tighten the drawstring securely. Cunning carp have a nasty habit of escaping a badly closed sack – Harry Houdini, eat your heart out!

The sacks I use have a very long retaining cord fitted to them, and this is what allows the carp to find a comfortable depth. Find a shady, deep margin, preferably with a bit of wind on it, and gently lower the carp into the water. They tend to stay on the surface for a while. Don't be alarmed by this, eventually they will drop down. Now secure the other end of the extension cord to a permanent fixture such as the boarding at the front of the swim. If nothing is available then use a bank stick, but please ensure it is well embedded. A powerful carp could make off with it if it is not secure. Once that

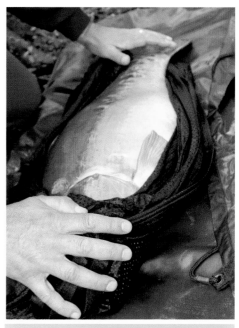

Ease the carp gently into a wet sack.

Secure the other end of the extension cord to a bank stick.

Before lifting a lively fish from the water, check that the fins are flush to the body.

It will take a little longer for the carp to settle down…

has happened, you are sentencing the fish to a very slow and lingering death. Please be very, very careful.

When it is time to retrieve the fish, pull it slowly towards you until it is on the surface. Remember, the carp will have had the opportunity to regain most if not all of its strength and will be very lively indeed. (This is one of the other reasons why I don't like to sack carp. On the unhooking mat, fully recovered, they can be something of a handful and that happens no matter what your level of experience is.) Before lifting the fish out, please ensure once again that the fins are lying flush to the body. The carp can now be taken to the unhooking mat. As I have said, it will take a little longer than usual for the carp to settle down but, once it has, you can get on with the pictures and then release it. Catching and handling a carp is a massive responsibility. Sacking one is even greater. Take every care and only do so if it is really necessary.

Returning

I don't know about anyone else, but I get the most tremendous satisfaction from seeing a fish swim off strongly after capture. It just seems to complete the whole picture for me. Although this is the final thing to do, we must still take every care. Never, and I mean never, pick up the fish and carry it back to the water. There is every danger that it will leap out of your hands and land heavily on the ground. The best way is either to use the weigh sling or wrap the fish up in the unhooking mat – always keeping it close to the ground. If the water in the margins is deep enough, then all you need do is place the fish in the edge and gently ease it into the water. Hold on to the wrist of the tail to support it in an upright position, and wait for it to swim off under its own steam. If, however, the fish starts to roll onto its side, then there will be no option other than to get in the water with it and hold it upright until it can support itself and swim away. You will also have to get into the water if the margins are shallow. Carp can damage themselves if they are allowed to flap over gravelly shallows. Make your way out until there is sufficient depth for the fish to swim away upright. Then the only thing left to do is have a celebratory cup of tea and tidy up the swim ready for the next one!

Transport the fish back to the water in the unhooking mat.

There is tremendous satisfaction at seeing a carp swim off strongly.

INDEX